AS YOU LIKE IT

By WILLIAM SHAKESPEARE

Preface and Annotations by
HENRY N. HUDSON

Introduction by
CHARLES HAROLD HERFORD

As You Like It
By William Shakespeare
Preface and Annotations by Henry N. Hudson
Introduction by Charles Harold Herford

Print ISBN 13: 978-1-4209-5410-4
eBook ISBN 13: 978-1-4209-5411-1

Cover Image: A detail of "Rosalind in the Forest," c. 1868 (oil on board), Sir John Everett Millais (1829-96) / © Walker Art Gallery, National Museums Liverpool / Bridgeman Images.

Please visit *www.digireads.com*

CONTENTS

ACT V.

Preface

Registered at the Stationers', in London, on the 4th of August, 1600. Two other of Shakespeare's plays, and one of Ben Jonson's, were entered at the same time; all of them under an injunction, "to be stayed." In regard to the other two of Shakespeare's plays, the stay appears to have been soon removed, as both of them were entered again in the course of the same month, and published before the end of that year. In the case of *As You Like It*, the stay seems to have been kept up; perhaps because its continued success on the stage made the theatrical company unwilling to part with their interest in it.

This is the only contemporary notice of the play that has been discovered. As it was not mentioned in the list given by Francis Meres in 1598, we are probably warranted in presuming it had not been heard of at that time. The play has a line, "Who ever loved, that loved not at first sight?" apparently quoted from Marlowe's version of *Hero and Leander*, which was published in 1598. So that we may safely conclude the play to have been written some time between that date and the date of the forecited entry at the Stationers'; that is, when the Poet was in his thirty-sixth or thirty-seventh year. The play was never printed, that we know of, till in the folio of 1623.

In regard to the originals of this play, two sources have been pointed out,—*The Cook's Tale of Gamelyn*, sometime attributed to Chaucer, but upon better advice excluded from his works; and a novel by Thomas Lodge entitled *Rosalynd; Euphues' Golden Legacy*. As the *Tale of Gamelyn* was not printed till more than a century later, it has been questioned whether Shakespeare ever saw it. Nor indeed can much be alleged as indicating that he ever did: one point there is, however, that may have some weight that way. An old knight, Sir John of Boundis, being about to die, calls in his wise friends to advise him touching the distribution of his property among his three sons. They advise him to settle all his lands on the eldest, and leave the youngest without any thing. Gamelyn, the youngest, being his favourite son, he rejects their advice, and bestows the largest portion upon him. The Poet goes much more according to their advice; Orlando, who answers to Gamelyn, having no share in the bulk of his father's estate. A few other resemblances, also, may be traced, wherein the play differs from Lodge's novel; though none of them are so strong as to force the inference that Shakespeare must have consulted the *Tale*.

Lodge's *Rosalynd* was first printed in 1590; and its popularity appears in that it was reprinted in 1592, and again in 1598. Steevens pronounced it a "worthless original"; but this sweeping sentence is so unjust as to breed some doubt whether he had read it. Compared with the general run of popular literature then in vogue, the novel has no little merit; and is very well entitled to the honour of having contributed to one of the most delightful poems ever written. A rather ambitious attempt indeed at fine writing; pedantic in style, not a little blemished with the elaborate euphemism of the time, and occasionally running into absurdity and indecorum; nevertheless, upon the whole, it is a varied and pleasing narrative, with passages of great force and beauty, and many touches of noble sentiment, and sometimes informed with a pastoral sweetness and simplicity quite charming.

To make a full sketch of the novel, in so far as the Poet borrowed from it, would occupy too much space. Still it seems desirable to indicate, somewhat, the extent of the Poet's obligations in this case; which can be best done, I apprehend, by stating, as compactly as may be, a portion of the story.

Sir John of Bordeaux, being at the point of death, called in his three sons, Saladyne, Fernandine, and Rosader, and divided his wealth among them, giving nearly a third to Rosader the youngest. After a short period of hypocritical mourning for his father, Saladyne went to studying how he might defraud his brothers, and ravish their legacies. He put Fernandine to school at Paris, and kept Rosader as his foot-boy. Rosader bore this patiently for three years, and then his spirit rose against it. While he was deep in meditation on the point, Saladyne came along and began to jerk him with rough speeches. After some interchange of angry and insulting words, Rosader "seized a great rake, and let drive at him," and soon brought him to terms. Saladyne, feigning sorrow for what he had done, then drew the youth, who was of a free and generous nature, into a reconciliation, till he might devise how to finish him out of the way.

Now, Gerismond, the rightful King of France, had been driven into exile, and his crown usurped, by Torismond, his younger brother. To amuse the people, and keep them from thinking of the banished King, the usurper appointed a day of wrestling and tournament; when a Norman, of great strength and stature, who had wrestled down as many as undertook with him, was to stand against all comers. Saladyne went to the Norman secretly, and engaged him with rich rewards to dispatch Rosader, in case Rosader should come within his grasp. He then pricked his brother on to the wrestling, telling him how much honour it would bring him, and that he was the only one to uphold the renown of the family. The youth, full of heroic thoughts, was glad of such an opportunity. When the time came, Torismond went to preside over the games, taking with him the Twelve Peers of France, his daughter Alinda, his niece Rosalynd, and all the most famous beauties of the Court. Rosalynd, "upon whose cheeks there seemed a battle between the graces," was the centre of attraction, "and made the Cavaliers crack their lances with more courage." The tournament being over, the Norman offered himself as general challenger at wrestling. While he is in the full career of success, Rosader alights from his horse, and presents himself for a trial. He quickly puts an end to the Norman's wrestling; though not till his eyes and thoughts have got badly entangled with the graces of Rosalynd. On the other side, she is equally smitten with his handsome person and heroic bearing, insomuch that, the spectacle being over, she takes from her neck a jewel, and sends it to him by a page, as an assurance of her favour.

This outline, as far as it goes, almost describes, word for word, the course and order of events in the play. And so it is, in a great measure, through the other parts and incidents of the plot; such as the usurper's banishment of his niece, and the escape of his daughter along with her; their arrival in the Forest of Arden, where Rosalynd's father has taken refuge; their encounter with the shepherds, their purchase of the cottage, and their adventures in the pastoral life. So, too, in the flight of Rosader to the same Forest, taking along with him the old servant, who is called Adam Spencer, his carving of love-verses in the bark of trees, his meeting with the disguised Rosalynd, and the wooing and marrying that enrich the forest scenes.

Thus much may suffice to show that the Poet has here borrowed a good deal of excellent matter. With what judgment and art the borrowed matter was used by him can only be understood on a careful study of his workmanship. In no one of his comedies indeed has he drawn more freely from others; nor, I may add, is there any one wherein he has enriched his drawings more liberally from the glory of his own genius. To appreciate his wisdom as shown in what he left unused, one must read the whole of Lodge's novel. In that work we find no traces of Jaques, or Touchstone, or Audrey; nothing, indeed, that could yield the slightest hint towards either of those characters. It scarce need be said that these superaddings are enough of themselves to transform the whole into another nature; pouring through all its veins a free and lively circulation of the most original wit and humour and poetry.

HENRY HUDSON

1880.

Introduction

As You Like It was first published in the Folio of 1623. A quarto edition contemplated in 1600 was 'staied' before publication,[1] and the inaccuracy of the Folio text favours the view that the printers had nothing but MS. before them,—probably one derived from the stage copy. No plausible reason for this 'staying' has been suggested. Mr. Wright (Clarendon Press edition, preface) dwells upon the marks of hasty execution,—the discrepancy about Rosalind's height, the gratuitous ambiguity of the two Jaques, the artless *dénoûment*,—and infers that Shakespeare sought to check the publication of his imperfect work. If he did so, he at least allowed it to remain imperfect .

The entry in the Stationers' Register is our one   Date of definite indication of the date. The play was probably written within the year preceding the entry (1599-1600); but the evidence is rather circumstantial than cogent. Meres does not mention it in his list (published autumn 1598). The famous allusion to Marlowe[2]— Shakespeare's only pointed and direct quotation from a contemporary—is probably, though not necessarily, later than the publication, in 1598, of his splendid version of *Hero and Leander*, where the dead shepherd's mighty saw is to be found. Closely akin in style to *Much Ado* and *Twelfth Night*, and not less blithe, it contains hints more distinct than either of the approach of a graver mood. Certainly, its laughter is less ringing, its humour more subtle and meditative; it is less rich in comic situations, but abounds in the more searching comedy of contrasted characters and views of life,—the comedy of Orlando's courtly flyting with Jaques, and Jaques's with Rosalind. The extremely uneventful stage-history of *As You Like It* shows that neither these qualities nor its exquisite romantic charm were, in general, found to compensate for its inferiority in downright comic power. Rosalind was not reckoned, with Beatrice and Malvolio and Falstaff, among the great comic creations of Shakespeare, which London of the next generation crowded to see.[3] Of early performances no record whatever remains, save the shadowy tradition, reported

---

[1] Stationers' Register, 4th August. Three other plays—*Much Ado, Henry V.*, and *Every Man in His Humour*—were stayed at the same time. The embargo on the first two was shortly removed (23rd August), and both were published,—one from an authentic text, the other surreptitiously and in a highly corrupt form.

[2]   'Dead shepherd, now I find
          thy saw of might;
     Whoever loved that loved
          not at first sight?'
                                        (iii. 5. 81.)

[3] L. Digges, lines prefixed to *Shakespeare's Poems*, 1640.

towards the end of the century by Oldys, that a younger brother of Shakespeare remembered once seeing him play 'a decrepit old man . . . supported and carried by another person to a table, at which he was seated among some company who were eating, and one of them sung a song'; evidently a reminiscence of Adam and Orlando in ii. 4. Apart from this, its history through the entire seventeenth century is a blank, and it probably passed altogether from the stage. When, in 1723, Charles Johnson undertook to revive its faded charms,[4] he took care to reinforce them with stimulating matter from other plays,—political speeches from *Richard II.*, misogyny from *Much Ado*, unconfessed love from *Twelfth Night*,—and to relieve them of all the pastoral scenes and of Touchstone. The original play was at length approximately restored in 1740; a series of great actresses—Mrs. Pritchard, Peg Woffington, Mrs. Jordan, Mrs. Siddons—found their opportunity in Rosalind, while Jaques and Touchstone were equally congenial roles to Quin. But it remained, on the whole, an actor's play. A finer appreciation of *As You Like It*, as of other romantic comedies, was reserved for the Romantic criticism of our century. It is interesting to note that, after holding, on the whole, an inconspicuous place among the romantic comedies of Shakespeare, it was singled out by the author of *La petite Fadette* as a means of introducing the French public to this—'the least popular, though often pillaged'—class of Shakespeare's work.[5]

Lodge's *Rosalynde*, or *Euphues' Golden Legacy*, the immediate source of the story of *As You Like It*, was one of the better specimens of the Pastoral Romances called forth by the vogue of the *Euphues* and the *Arcadia*,—a highly artificial and composite genre which already, in 1600, was visibly touched with decay. The ornate Euphuistic conversation which Lodge and Greene put in the mouths of their Arcadians, had yielded in real life to later affectations. The courtly and bookish pastoralism of Sidney and Spenser was passing into a sentiment more akin to the modern delight in nature, and fostering a like watchfulness of natural life,—the pastoralism of Drayton and Browne and Wither. Unreal as it was, however, the earlier Elizabethan pastoralism had seldom been strictly Arcadian. Sidney, like his predecessor Montemayor, had loved to disturb the shepherd's piping with the alarms of war, and rarely allowed his readers to forget that Arcadia marched with Sparta. And Lodge, a soldier and a sailor, who wrote his romance 'in ocean, when everie line was wet with a surge,' was not the man to let the tradition die. He drew his secluded Arden with one eye upon the Arcady of literature, and the other upon the

---

[4] *Love in a Forest.*
[5] George Sand, *Comme Il vous Plaira* (1856). Cf. her instructive preface. She adapts with a freedom not unwarranted in her case.

Sherwood of Robin Hood. Sidney transports us on the first page into the shepherdworld: Lodge lingers, with evident gusto, over the preliminary exploits and perils of his hero. These he took from the rude fourteenth-century romance of *Gamelyn*, handed down in several MSS. of the *Canterbury Tales* as the Tale of the Cook, and possibly intended by Chaucer as material for the Tale of the Yeoman. It is a lay of family feud, artless in form, but full of hearty English vigour and the relish of hard blows. Gamelyn's elder brother, bent on getting rid of him, persuades him to challenge a famous wrestler. Gamelyn is victorious, and proceeds, by way of vengeance, to lay siege to his brother's house with an armed band. At first successful, he is taken prisoner, but released by an old servant, Adam Spenser, with whom he flies to the forest. This opening adventure Lodge takes over with little change, and sets in a romantic framework of his own. Rosader (Gamelyn) and his brother Saladyn have a counterpart in the banished king Gerismond and the usurper Torismond. Rosader wrestles before Torismond, slays the king's wrestler, and wins the love of Rosalind. Torismond presently, on a trifling pretext, banishes Rosalind from court, and when Alinda, his daughter, takes her part, she is banished too. Both fly, like Rosader, to the paradise of exiles in Arden. But Arden has its own inhabitants also; some of them of the pure Arcadian breed,—Montanus who laments, and Phoebe who will not listen; others, like the old shepherd Corydon, akin rather to the Spenserian breed of quasi-rustic Hobbinols, whose speech is larded with uncouth terms without becoming thereby more like life. In this artificial world Rosalind (Ganimede) appropriately unfolds the gay diplomacy which leads, as in the play, to the marriage of three pairs of true lovers. Pastoral peace is not entirely preserved: a robber-band threatens Alinda,and Rosader rescues her; a lion threatens Saladyn, and Rosader slays it. But country simplicity, subtle humour, and meditative refinement are absent; there is no hint of William and Audrey, none of Jaques, none of Touchstone.

Lodge had essayed to correct the monotony of Pastoral romance by bold infusions of alien matter, controlled by a taste decidedly immature. The result was a medley in which the mediaeval and the Elizabethan, the yeoman and the courtly, elements are intermingled but not interfused. In Shakespeare's hands the story, far from being simplified, acquired a richer and more varied relation to life, and reflected the hues of contemporary humour and affectation from a thousand brilliant facets of which there is no hint in Lodge; yet in none of the comedies do we find a more finished and gracious harmony of tone, or, with so much that is recognisable in detail, a total effect so new. Here, if anywhere, we have Shakespearean Romance,—men and women vital and human to the core, moving in a world fantastical, evanescent, dreamlike. 'If you like it, so!' Lodge had written to the gentlemen readers of his *Rosalind*; and Shakespeare modelled on the phrase a title which archly deprecates any claim to grave significance in his work. Without any laborious moulding or studious trimming of excrescences, the whole has fallen into scale and proportion, and the discrepant materials, without any loss of individual piquancy, are touched into delicate accord. The story itself he took over with a few changes, which make the forest life in Arden more obviously its central theme. Spenser had already flung a glamour of romance over Arden,—

> So wide a forest and so waste as this
> Nor famous Ardeyn nor fowle Arlo is;

he had sung in *Astrophel*; and Lodge had introduced romantic details,—*e.g.* the lion; characteristically, however, impairing the romantic effect by giving his Arden a definite locality, between Lyon and Bordeaux (p. 86). Shakespeare's Arden is at once more fantastic and more real. Its geography is as vague as the date of the usurping and banished 'duke.' Its inmates live an idyllic life,—'fleeting the time carelessly as they did in the golden world,' exempt from privation or alarm. Its security is threatened by no robbers such as Lodge permitted to seize Alinda; and the duke, unlike Lodge's Gerismond, is precluded from all anxiety about the fate of Rosalind until he sees her, for he is unaware of her banishment. But the picture is full of the detailed touches and the atmosphere caught from the greenwood and the chase,—familiar memories of the Warwickshire Arden happily mingling with the fables of Ardennes. The inmates of Arden are still more composite than the landscape. They form three groups, distinguished not so much by the characters that compose them as by the different quality of the atmosphere through which they are viewed. Phoebe, Audrey, and Rosalind do not merely represent different phases of the real world, they stand in different relations to reality. Phœbe and Silvius move, like their prototypes, in the artificial glamour of literary pastoral, in an atmosphere charged with sentiment and almost devoid of observation. In Corin, on the other hand, the faint incipient realism of Lodge's Corydon is skilfully heightened, and that rustic in embryo becomes an admirable study of the sententious old shepherd of real life. His name associates Corin with the Arcadians, Phoebe and Silvius; but his character consorts him with the homelier couple, William and Audrey, the goatherd of Shakespeare's invention, who represent the naïveté of the English rustic without any softening charm.

A far subtler transformation has befallen the courtly denizens of Arden, who in Lodge belong to literary Pastoral like the rest, but in Shakespeare mediate exquisitely between reality and romance. They, again, form two sub-groups which at moments meet and scintillate, but do not mingle till the close,—the banished duke and his lords, and Rosalind and Orlando. The exhilaration of free woodland life, which is one of the ultimate springs of all Pastoral, has entered into both; but in the duke it begets a benign philosophy, in Rosalind exuberant humour. Both Rosalind and Orlando retain an outward resemblance to their conventional prototypes. Both pursue their loves by the fantastic devices of Pastoral; Orlando mars the trees with sonnets, and Rosalind wins him by feigning the truth. But these fantastic elements are drawn within the sphere of human nature by virtue, above all, of the delightful character of Rosalind herself,—an original blend of playfulness and passion. A less ardent Rosalind would have shown less enterprise in her love; a duller or a graver one would have been less ingeniously indirect in its execution. The lyric apostrophes of Juliet are only an exquisite form of the conventional speech of love-rapture; Rosalind's speech is from first to last absolutely individual, a love-language entirely her own, and lending itself to the utterance of no other tongue. The exquisite lyrics of Lodge's *Rosalind* were necessarily lost.

Lodge's Rosader—half ruffler, half sentimental shepherd— presented a perhaps more difficult problem. It is in his story that Shakespeare has made most changes, especially in the part of it which Lodge drew most directly from *Gamelyn*. Orlando is the nearest approach in Shakespeare to the fresh young knight of chivalry, or to such a figure as Chaucer's Squier, steeped in the romance of the woods and of love. He has lost both the rustic simplicity of Rosader and his rustic violence. He neither loses his senses under the spell of Rosalind's beauty, nor brings a posse of roysterers to batter his brother's door. His character, like his name, is caught from the traditions of a highbred and courtly valour, heightened by the peculiarly Shakespearean trait that it springs rather from race than from training, for his brother has neglected their father's charge—to bring him up in 'all gentlemanlike qualities.'[6] His father's spirit triumphs over his 'peasant' training, as it does in Arviragus and Guiderius and Perdita, though the psychological subtlety shown in tracing the conflict of birth and breeding in the *Winter's Tale* is wholly wanting in the earlier creation. In keeping with the fine *cortesia* communicated to the figure of Orlando, the whole plot has been lifted into a blither atmosphere. Tragic harms still loom on the horizon, but they rouse no foreboding, and approach only to disperse. Their contrivers, Oliver and Frederick, are from the first less grave offenders than their prototypes, and they repent on yet slighter

---

[6] In this prescription, as in one or two other points, the play resembles *Gamelyn* and diverges from Lodge. Whether Shakespeare knew *Gamelyn* has, in consequence, been warmly debated. The question must remain undecided. The resemblances are not marked enough to compel the assumption (made by Knight, Grey, Upton), but they suggest it; and it is rash to assume that what Lodge certainly knew cannot have been known to Shakespeare. Lodge probably read the MS. in some Oxford library, but the close correspondences of his version suggest that he had made a copy or notes. The negative view has been closely argued by Delius (*Jahrbuch*, vi. 247 f.) and Zupitza (ib. xxi. 93 f.).

provocation.[7] Even Charles the wrestler is stunned, not slain.

It is to this third group—the courtly inmates of Arden—that Shakespeare has made his most important original additions. Touchstone and Jaques, profoundly as they differ, stand in a somewhat similar relation to the sub-groups to whom they are directly attached. Touchstone is the foil to Rosalind's humour, Jaques to the duke's philosophy; Touchstone parodies Orlando's verses, Jaques Amiens's song; Touchstone is the court-jester, Jaques 'has a mind to the same office, and thinks motley the only wear.' Something of Shakespeare's early symmetry of design lingers in the mode of their introduction into the plot: Touchstone has followed Celia into exile, Jaques the duke; and both relations are probably modelled on the devotion of old Adam to Orlando,—a trait retained from the oldest extant form of the story. Both represent a new departure in Shakespeare's dramatic technique. In Touchstone he for the first time utilised the professional court-fool as a medium of wit and humour. In Jaques he for the first time introduced a character of the first rank, whose entire role is that of the contemplative observer. Both figures are set like boulders in the pellucid stream of the drama, contributing nothing to its movement, but making its hidden tendencies, its currents and cross-currents, visible and explicit. The contrasts of court and country, of society and nature, which the other persons embody but hardly express, are forced into prominence by the dry jests of the ex-court fool and the biting sarcasms of the disillusioned worldling. Touchstone is a shrewd rustic who has served at court, and armed himself with its accomplishments, without foregoing his native blunt humour. He conveys his buffooneries through the formulas of courtly wit. He makes game of the simplicity of Corin and Audrey, and parodies the 'strange capers' of the courtly lovers. Jaques's relations with the rustics are of the slightest, but he serves as a most effective foil for the courtiers. His philosophy is a sort of heightened and distorted version of the duke's, and the duke despises his character but loves his company. If the duke sighs over the stricken stag, Jaques moralises its fate into a thousand similes; if the duke makes a passing comparison of the world to a stage, Jaques follows it up with the famous 'seven ages of man.' If Touchstone is allowed a momentary advantage over Orlando and Rosalind, the fresh and robust good-nature of the one and the buoyant wit of the other are far more emphatically opposed (in two nearly adjacent scenes, iii. i. and iv. i.) to Jaques's cynical gloom. 'Will you sit down with me? We two will rail

---

[7] Frederick, though slightly sketched, is more intelligible than Torismond. It was an admirable stroke to make him the brother of the rightful duke. This makes more natural his retention of Rosalind at his court after her father's banishment, and introduces a telling parallelism between him and Oliver. Torismond, with the insensate fury of the stage-despot, banishes his daughter as well as his niece; Celia's flight is the beginning of Frederick's repentance.

against our mistress the world,'—is his invitation to Orlando. 'I will chide no breather in the world but myself, in whom I know most faults.'

Jaques has clearly morbid traits; yet he represents a type very characteristic of the early seventeenth century, and one which, as the minute and elaborate drawing shows, greatly interested Shakespeare. The staple of his 'melancholy' was the vague sadness of a sated brain, the despondent waking after the glorious national revelry of Elizabeth's prime. But there are glimpses in it of a profounder and nobler melancholy, which Shakespeare himself, it can hardly be doubted, came to share, melancholy of a profound sensitiveness to wrong and to suffering. Jaques's effusive pathos over the wounded stag, strange and untimely note as it sounds among the blithe horns and carols of the hunters, preludes a deeper, more comprehensive pity,—the stuff of which, in the next years, the great tragedies were to be wrought.

CHARLES HAROLD HERFORD

1902.

AS YOU LIKE IT

Dramatis Personae

DUKE, *living in exile*
FREDERICK, *Brother to the Duke, and Usurper of his Dominions*
AMIENS, *Lord attending on the Duke in his Banishment*
JAQUES, *Lord attending on the Duke in his Banishment*
LE BEAU, *a Courtier attending upon Frederick*
CHARLES, *his Wrestler*
OLIVER, *Son of Sir Rowland de Bois*
JAQUES, *Son of Sir Rowland de Bois*
ORLANDO, *Son of Sir Rowland de Bois*
ADAM, *Servant to Oliver*
DENNIS, *Servant to Oliver*
TOUCHSTONE, *a Clown*
SIR OLIVER MARTEXT, *a Vicar*
CORIN, *Shepherd*
SILVIUS, *Shepherd*
WILLIAM, *a Country Fellow, in love with Audrey*
A person representing HYMEN, *god of marriage*

ROSALIND, *Daughter to the banished Duke*
CELIA, *Daughter to Frederick*
PHEBE, *a Shepherdess*
AUDREY, *a Country Wench*

Lords belonging to the two Dukes;
Pages, Foresters, and other Attendants.

The Scene lies first near OLIVER's *house; afterwards partly in the Usurper's court and partly in the Forest of Arden.*

ACT I.

SCENE I.

OLIVER's *Orchard.*

[*Enter* ORLANDO *and* ADAM.]

ORLANDO. As I remember, Adam, it was upon this fashion,—bequeathed me by will but poor a[8] thousand crowns, and, as thou say'st, charged my brother, on his blessing, to breed me well: and there begins my sadness. My brother Jaques[9] he keeps at school, and report speaks goldenly of his profit: for my part, he keeps me rustically at home, or, to speak more properly, stays me here at home unkept: for call you that keeping for a gentleman of my birth that differs not from the stalling of an ox? His horses are bred better; for, besides that they are fair with their feeding, they are taught their manage,[10] and to that end riders dearly hired; but I, his brother, gain nothing under him but growth; for the which his animals on his dunghills are as much bound to him as I. Besides this nothing that he so plentifully gives me, the something that nature gave me, his countenance[11] seems to take from me: he lets me feed with his hinds, bars me the place of a brother, and as much as in him lies, mines my gentility[12] with my education. This is it, Adam, that grieves me; and the spirit of my father, which I think is within me, begins to mutiny against this servitude; I will no longer endure it, though yet I know no wise remedy how to avoid it.

ADAM. Yonder comes my master, your brother.

ORLANDO. Go apart, Adam, and thou shalt hear how he will shake me up. [ADAM *retires.*]

[*Enter* OLIVER.]

---

[8] Such was the usage of the time. We have like forms of speech in *good my lord, sweet my coz, gentle my brother, dear my sister,* and many others.—"*On* his blessing," in the next line, means *as the condition* of his blessing.

[9] Shakespeare and other dramatists of his time use *Jaques* as a dissyllable, and, wherever the name occurs in their verse, the metre requires it to be pronounced so.

[10] *Manage* was used for the training, breaking, or educating of a horse to obey the hand and voice.

[11] *Countenance,* here, is *treatment* or *entertainment.* Well explained in Selden's *Table Talk:* "The old law was, that when a man was fined, he was to be fined *salvo contenemento,* so as his countenance might be safe; taking *countenance* in the same sense as your countryman does when he says, if you will come to my house, I will show you the best countenance I can; that is not the best face, but the best *entertainment.*"

[12] *Mines* for *undermines,* and *gentility* for *noble birth.* So that the meaning is, "What an honourable parentage has done for me, he strives to undo by base breeding."

OLIVER. Now, sir! what make you here?[13]

ORLANDO. Nothing: I am not taught to make anything.

OLIVER. What mar you then, sir?

ORLANDO. Marry,[14] sir, I am helping you to mar that which God made, a poor unworthy brother of yours, with idleness.

OLIVER. Marry, sir, be better employed, and be naught awhile![15]

ORLANDO. Shall I keep your hogs, and eat husks with them? What prodigal portion[16] have I spent that I should come to such penury?

OLIVER. Know you where you are, sir?

ORLANDO. O, sir, very well: here in your orchard.

OLIVER. Know you before whom, sir?

ORLANDO. Ay, better than him I am before knows me. I know you are my eldest brother: and in the gentle condition of blood, you should so know me. The courtesy of nations allows you my better in that you are the first-born; but the same tradition takes not away my blood, were there twenty brothers betwixt us: I have as much of my father in me as you, albeit; I confess, your coming before me is nearer to his reverence.[17]

OLIVER. What, boy!

ORLANDO. Come, come, elder brother, you are too young in this.[18]

OLIVER. Wilt thou lay hands on me, villain?

ORLANDO. I am no villain: I am the youngest son of Sir Rowland de Bois: he was my father; and he is thrice a villain that says such a father begot villains. Wert thou not my brother, I would not take this hand from thy throat till this other had pulled out thy tongue for saying so: thou has railed on thyself.

ADAM. [*Coming forward.*] Sweet masters, be patient; for your father's remembrance, be at accord.

OLIVER. Let me go, I say.

ORLANDO. I will not, till I please: you shall hear me. My father charged you in his will to give me good education: you have trained me like a peasant, obscuring and hiding from me all

---

[13] "What *make* you here?" is old language for "what *are* you *doing* here?" A very frequent usage.

[14] *Marry* was used a good deal in colloquial language as a petty oath or intensive; something like the Latin *heracle* and *edepol*. This use of *marry* sprang from a custom of swearing by St. Mary the Virgin.

[15] *Be naught*, or *go and be naught*, was formerly a petty execration between anger and contempt, which has been supplanted by others, as *be hanged, be cursed*, &c.; *awhile*, or *the while*, was added merely to round the phrase.

[16] The allusion to the parable of the Prodigal Son is obvious enough.

[17] Nearer to him in the right of that reverence which was his due.

[18] The word *boy* naturally provokes and awakens in Orlando the sense of his manly powers; and, with the retort of *elder* brother, he grasps him with firm hands, and makes him feel he is no boy. So in Lodge's story: "Though I am *eldest* by birth, yet, never having attempted any deeds of arms, I am *youngest* to perform any martial exploits."

gentleman-like qualities.[19] The spirit of my father grows strong in
me, and I will no longer endure it: therefore, allow me such
exercises as may become a gentleman, or give me the poor
allottery[20] my father left me by testament; with that I will go buy
my fortunes.

OLIVER. And what wilt thou do? beg, when that is spent? Well, sir,
get you in; I will not long be troubled with you: you shall have
some part of your will: I pray you leave me.

ORLANDO. I no further offend you than becomes me for my good.

OLIVER. Get you with him, you old dog.

ADAM. Is *old dog* my reward? Most true, I have lost my teeth in your
service.—God be with my old master! he would not have spoke
such a word.

[*Exeunt* ORLANDO *and* ADAM.]

OLIVER. Is it even so? begin you to grow upon me? I will physic your
rankness,[21] and yet give no thousand crowns neither.—Holla,
Dennis!

[*Enter* DENNIS.]

DENNIS. Calls your worship?

OLIVER. Was not Charles, the Duke's wrestler, here to speak with
me?

DENNIS. So please you, he is here at the door and importunes access
to you.

OLIVER. Call him in. [*Exit* DENNIS.]—'Twill be a good way; and to-
morrow the wrestling is.

[*Enter* CHARLES.]

CHARLES. Good morrow to your worship.

OLIVER. Good Monsieur Charles!—what's the new news at the new
court?

CHARLES. There's no news at the court, sir, but the old news; that is,
the old Duke is banished by his younger brother the new Duke; and
three or four loving lords have put themselves into voluntary exile
with him, whose lands and revenues enrich the new Duke;

---

[19] *Qualities* here probably means *pursuits* or *occupations*; thus according with
exercises a little after. The Poet often uses *quality so.*

[20] *Allotery* is *portion*; that which is *allotted.*

[21] *Rankness* is *overgrowth*, or having too much blood in him. Oliver's thought is,
that Orlando is growing too big for his station, and so needs to be taken down. The Poet
repeatedly uses to *physic* for to *heal.*

therefore he gives them good leave to wander.

OLIVER. Can you tell if Rosalind, the Duke's daughter, be banished with her father?

CHARLES. O, no; for the Duke's daughter, her cousin, so loves her,—being ever from their cradles bred together,—that she would have followed her exile, or have died to stay[22] behind her. She is at the court, and no less beloved of her uncle than his own daughter; and never two ladies loved as they do.

OLIVER. Where will the old Duke live?

CHARLES. They say he is already in the Forest of Arden,[23] and a many merry men with him; and there they live like the old Robin Hood[24] of England: they say many young gentlemen flock to him every day, and fleet the time carelessly,[25] as they did in the golden world.[26]

OLIVER. What, you wrestle to-morrow before the new Duke?

CHARLES. Marry, do I, sir; and I came to acquaint you with a matter. I am given, sir, secretly to understand that your younger brother, Orlando, hath a disposition to come in disguis'd against me to try a fall. To-morrow, sir, I wrestle for my credit; and he that escapes me without some broken limb shall[27] acquit him well. Your brother is but young and tender; and, for your love, I would be loath to foil him, as I must, for my own honour, if he come in: therefore, out of my love to you, I came hither to acquaint you withal; that either you might stay him from his intendment, or brook such disgrace well as he shall run into; in that it is thing of his own search, and altogether against my will.

OLIVER. Charles, I thank thee for thy love to me, which thou shalt find I will most kindly requite. I had myself notice of my brother's purpose herein, and have by underhand means laboured to dissuade him from it; but he is resolute. I'll tell thee, Charles, it is the stubbornest young fellow of France; full of ambition, an envious

---

[22] *To stay* is an instance of the infinitive used gerundively, or like the Latin *gerund*, and so is equivalent to *by* or *from staying*. The usage is very frequent in Shakespeare, and sometimes makes his meaning obscure.

[23] *Ardenne* was a large forest in French Flanders, lying near the river Meuse, and between Charlemont and Rocroy.

[24] This prince of outlaws and "most gentle theefe" lived in the time of Richard I., and had his chief residence in Sherwood Forest, Nottinghamshire. Wordsworth aptly styles him "the English ballad-singer's joy"; and in Percy's *Reliques* is an old ballad entitled *Robin Head and Guy of Gisborne*, showing how his praises were wont to be sung. His character and mode of life are well delivered in Scott's *Ivanhoe*.

[25] *Carelessly* is used elegantly here, in the sense of *freedom from care*.

[26] Of this fabled golden age,—an ancient and very general tradition wherein the state of man in Paradise appears to have been shadowed,—some notion is given in Gonzalo's Commonwealth, *The Tempest*, Act ii., scene 1.

[27] *Shall* for *will*. The two were often used indiscriminately. "Will have to *do his best*" is the meaning. *Him* for *himself*, of course.

emulator of every man's good parts, a secret and villainous
contriver against me his natural brother: therefore use thy
discretion: I had as lief thou didst break his neck as his finger.
And thou wert best look to't; for if thou dost him any slight disgrace, or
if he do not mightily grace himself on thee,[28] he will practise
against thee by poison, entrap thee by some treacherous device,
and never leave thee till he hath ta'en thy life by some indirect
means or other: for, I assure thee, and almost with tears I speak it,
there is not one so young and so villainous this day living. I speak
but brotherly of him; but should I anatomize[29] him to thee as he is,
I must blush and weep, and thou must look pale and wonder.

CHARLES. I am heartily glad I came hither to you. If he come to-
morrow I'll give him his payment:[30] if ever he go alone again I'll
never wrestle for prize more: and so, God keep your worship!

OLIVER. Farewell, good Charles. [*Exit* CHARLES.]—Now will I stir
this gamester:[31] I hope I shall see an end of him: for my soul, yet I
know not why, hates nothing more than he. Yet he's gentle; never
schooled and yet learned; full of noble device; of all sorts
enchantingly beloved; and, indeed, so much in the heart of the
world, and especially of my own people, who best know him, that I
am altogether misprised: but it shall not be so long; this wrestler
shall clear all: nothing remains but that I kindle[32] the boy thither,
which now I'll go about. [*Exit.*]

SCENE II.

A Lawn before the DUKE's *Palace.*

[*Enter* ROSALIND *and* CELIA.]

CELIA. I pray thee, Rosalind, sweet my coz, be merry.

ROSALIND. Dear Celia, I show more mirth than I am mistress of; and
would you yet I were merrier? Unless you could teach me to forget
a banished father, you must not learn me how to remember any
extraordinary pleasure.

CELIA. Herein I see thou lov'st me not with the full weight that I love
thee; if my uncle, thy banished father, had banished thy uncle, the

---

[28] That is, "get himself honour or reputation at your expense."

[29] To *anatomize*, as the word is here used, is to unfold, explain, or expose a thing
thoroughly. Burton's *Anatomy of Melancholy* is a capital instance in point. The same
sense survives in the technical use of the word in Medical Science.

[30] *Payment* for *punishment*. The verb *to pay* is often so used.

[31] *Gamester* was used very much as our phrase *sporting character*, or of one sowing
his wild oats.

[32] Spur him on. So in *Macbeth*: "That, trusted home, might yet *enkindle* you unto
the crown."

Duke my father, so thou hadst been still with me, I could have taught my love to take thy father for mine; so wouldst thou, if the truth of thy love to me were so righteously tempered as mine is to thee.

ROSALIND. Well, I will forget the condition of my estate, to rejoice in yours.

CELIA. You know my father hath no child but I,[33] nor none is like to have; and, truly, when he dies thou shalt be his heir: for what he hath taken away from thy father perforce, I will render thee again in affection: by mine honour, I will; and when I break that oath, let me turn monster; therefore, my sweet Rose, my dear Rose, be merry.

ROSALIND. From henceforth I will, coz, and devise sports: let me see; what think you of falling in love?

CELIA. Marry, I pr'ythee, do, to make sport withal: but love no man in good earnest, nor no further in sport neither than with safety of a pure blush thou mayst in honour come off again.

ROSALIND. What shall be our sport, then?

CELIA. Let us sit and mock the good housewife Fortune from her wheel,[34] that her gifts may henceforth be bestowed equally.

ROSALIND. I would we could do so; for her benefits are mightily misplaced: and the bountiful blind woman doth most mistake in her gifts to women.

CELIA. 'Tis true; for those that she makes fair she scarce makes honest; and those that she makes honest she makes very ill-favouredly.

ROSALIND. Nay; now thou goest from Fortune's office to Nature's: Fortune reigns in gifts of the world, not in the lineaments of Nature.

[*Enter* TOUCHSTONE.]

CELIA. No; when Nature hath made a fair creature, may she not by Fortune fall into the fire?—Though Nature hath given us wit to flout at Fortune, hath not Fortune sent in this Fool to cut off the argument?

ROSALIND. Indeed, there is Fortune too hard for Nature, when Fortune makes Nature's natural[35] the cutter-off of Nature's wit.

CELIA. Peradventure this is not Fortune's work neither, but Nature's, who perceiveth our natural wits too dull to reason of such

---

[33] In the unsettled grammar of Shakespeare's time, such a misplacing of the cases, as compared with present usage, was quite common even with the best-educated people.

[34] That is, drive her from it with gibes and flouts.

[35] *Natural* was used, as it still is, like *innocent*, for a veritable fool. The application of *fool* to the professional clown gave rise to many quibbles.

goddesses, and hath sent this natural for our whetstone: for always the dullness of the Fool is the whetstone of the wits.—How now, wit? whither wander you?

TOUCHSTONE. Mistress, you must come away to your father.

CELIA. Were you made the messenger?

TOUCHSTONE. No, by mine honour; but I was bid to come for you.

ROSALIND. Where learned you that oath, Fool?

TOUCHSTONE. Of a certain knight that swore by his honour they were good pancakes, and swore by his honour the mustard was naught:[36] now, I'll stand to it, the pancakes were naught and the mustard was good: and yet was not the knight forsworn.

CELIA. How prove you that, in the great heap of your knowledge?

ROSALIND. Ay, marry; now unmuzzle your wisdom.

TOUCHSTONE. Stand you both forth now: stroke your chins, and swear by your beards that I am a knave.

CELIA. By our beards, if we had them, thou art.

TOUCHSTONE. By my knavery, if I had it, then I were: but if you swear by that that is not, you are not forsworn: no more was this knight, swearing by his honour, for he never had any; or if he had, he had sworn it away before ever he saw those pancackes or that mustard.

CELIA. Pr'ythee, who is't that thou mean'st?

TOUCHSTONE. One that old[37] Frederick, your father, loves.

CELIA. My father's love is enough to honour him enough: speak no more of him; you'll be whipp'd for taxation[38] one of these days.

TOUCHSTONE. The more pity that fools may not speak wisely what wise men do foolishly.

CELIA. By my troth, thou sayest true: for since the little wit that fools have was silenced, the little foolery that wise men have makes a great show.—Here comes Monsieur Le Beau.

ROSALIND. With his mouth full of news.

CELIA. Which he will put on us as pigeons feed their young.

ROSALIND. Then shall we be news-crammed.

CELIA. All the better; we shall be the more marketable.—

[*Enter* LE BEAU.]

Bon jour, Monsieur Le Beau. What's the news?

---

[36] *Naught* is simply *bad*, as in our word *naughty*. It must not be confounded with *nought*.

[37] *Old* is here merely a term of familiarity, such as Fools were privileged to use to and of all sorts of people.

[38] It was the custom to whip Fools when they used their tongues too freely. *Taxation* is *censure, satire*. So in ii. 7, of this play: "Why, who cries out on pride, that can therein *tax* any private party?"

LE BEAU. Fair princess, you have lost much good sport.

CELIA. Sport! of what colour?[39]

LE BEAU. What colour, madam? How shall I answer you?

ROSALIND. As wit and fortune will.

TOUCHSTONE. Or as the destinies decrees.

CELIA. Well said: that was laid on with a trowel.[40]

TOUCHSTONE. Nay, if I keep not my rank,—

ROSALIND. Thou losest thy old smell.

LE BEAU. You amaze me, ladies; I would have told you of good wrestling, which you have lost the sight of.

ROSALIND. Yet tell us the manner of the wrestling.

LE BEAU. I will tell you the beginning, and, if it please your ladyships, you may see the end; for the best is yet to do; and here, where you are, they are coming to perform it.

CELIA. Well,—the beginning, that is dead and buried.

LE BEAU. There comes an old man and his three sons,—

CELIA. I could match this beginning with an old tale.

LE BEAU.—three proper[41] young men, of excellent growth and presence, with bills on their necks;[42]—

ROSALIND. *Be it known unto all men by these presents.*

LE BEAU.—the eldest of the three wrestled with Charles, the Duke's wrestler; which Charles in a moment threw him, and broke three of his ribs, that there is little hope of life in him: so he served the second, and so the third. Yonder they lie; the poor old man, their father, making such pitiful dole over them that all the beholders take his part with weeping.

ROSALIND. Alas!

TOUCHSTONE. But what is the sport, monsieur, that the ladies have lost?

LE BEAU. Why, this that I speak of.

TOUCHSTONE. Thus men may grow wiser every day! It is the first time that ever I heard breaking of ribs was sport for ladies.

CELIA. Or I, I promise thee.

---

[39] Celia glances, apparently, at La Beau's affected or dandified pronunciation of *sport*, he having got it nearer to *spot* than to *sport*.

[40] This is a proverbial phrase, meaning to do any thing without delicacy, or to *lay it on thick*. If a man flatter grossly, it is common to say, *he lays it on with a trowel*. The *Destinies* shape the speech of those who have not sense enough to shape it for themselves.

[41] *Proper* is *handsome* or *fine-looking*. Commonly so in Shakespeare.

[42] *Bills* were instruments or weapons used by watchmen and foresters. Watchmen were said to carry their bills or halberds on their *necks*, not on their shoulders. There is a quibble on the word *bills*, in the next speech, referring to public notices, which were generally headed with the words,—"Be it known unto all men by these presents."

ROSALIND. But is there any else longs to see this broken music[43] in his sides? is there yet another dotes upon rib-breaking?—Shall we see this wrestling, cousin?

LE BEAU. You must, if you stay here: for here is the place appointed for the wrestling, and they are ready to perform it.

CELIA. Yonder, sure, they are coming: let us now stay and see it.

[*Flourish. Enter* DUKE FREDERICK, LORDS, ORLANDO, CHARLES, *and* Attendants.]

DUKE FREDERICK. Come on; since the youth will not be entreated, his own peril on his forwardness.

ROSALIND. Is yonder the man?

LE BEAU. Even he, madam.

CELIA. Alas, he is too young: yet he looks successfully.[44]

DUKE FREDERICK. How now, daughter and cousin![45] are you crept hither to see the wrestling?

ROSALIND. Ay, my liege; so please you give us leave.

DUKE FREDERICK. You will take little delight in it, I can tell you, there is such odds in the men. In pity of the challenger's youth I would fain dissuade him, but he will not be entreated.[46] Speak to him, ladies; see if you can move him.

CELIA. Call him hither, good Monsieur Le Beau.

DUKE FREDERICK. Do so; I'll not be by. [*The* DUKE *goes apart.*]

LE BEAU. Monsieur the challenger, the princesses call for you.

ORLANDO. I attend them with all respect and duty.

ROSALIND. Young man, have you challenged Charles the wrestler?

ORLANDO. No, fair Princess; he is the general challenger: I come but

---

[43] What sort of music was meant by this phrase, has been much in doubt. Chappell, in his *Popular Music of the Olden Time*, says the phrase "means what we now term *a string* band." But he has since changed his opinion, and his later explanation, given to Mr. W. A. Wright, Editor of the "Clarendon Press Series," is as follows: "Some instruments, such as viols, violins, flutes, &c., were formerly made in sets of four, which when played together formed a *consort*. If one or more of the instruments of one set were substituted for the corresponding ones of another set, the result was no longer a *consort* but *broken music*." The expression occurs in *Henry V.*, v. 2: "Come, your answer in broken music; for thy voice is music, and thy English broken." And Bacon, Essay xxxvii.: "I understand it, that the Song be in Quire, placed aloft, and accompanied with some broken Musicke."—The implied comparison of *broken ribs* to *broken music* appears to be but a whimsical fancy, with no link of connection but a verbal one suggested by *broken.*

[44] "Looks *successful,*" or as one *likely to succeed.* The Poet has repeated instances of adverbs thus used as adjectives, as also *vice versa.*

[45] *Cousin* was used indifferently of nephews, nieces, and grandchildren, as well as for what we mean by the term. Shakespeare is full of instances in point. Rosalind is *niece* to Frederick.

[46] This phrase has occurred just before, and of course means "will not yield to entreaty," or "will not be prevailed upon."

in, as others do, to try with him the strength of my youth.

CELIA. Young gentleman, your spirits are too bold for your years. You have seen cruel proof of this man's strength: if you saw yourself with your eyes, or knew yourself with your judgment, the fear of your adventure would counsel you to a more equal enterprise. We pray you, for your own sake, to embrace your own safety and give over this attempt.

ROSALIND. Do, young sir; your reputation shall not therefore be misprised:[47] we will make it our suit to the Duke that the wrestling might not go forward.

ORLANDO. I beseech you, punish me not with your hard thoughts: wherein I confess me much guilty to deny[48] so fair and excellent ladies anything. But let your fair eyes and gentle wishes go with me to my trial: wherein if I be foiled there is but one shamed that was never gracious;[49] if killed, but one dead that is willing to be so: I shall do my friends no wrong, for I have none to lament me: the world no injury, for in it I have nothing; only in the world I fill up a place, which may be better supplied when I have made it empty.

ROSALIND. The little strength that I have, I would it were with you.

CELIA. And mine to eke out hers.

ROSALIND. Fare you well. Pray Heaven, I be deceived in you!

CELIA. Your heart's desires be with you.

CHARLES. Come, where is this young gallant that is so desirous to lie with his mother earth?

ORLANDO. Ready, sir; but his will hath in it a more modest working.

DUKE FREDERICK. You shall try but one fall.

CHARLES. No; I warrant your grace, you shall not entreat him to a second, that have so mightily persuaded him from a first.

ORLANDO. You mean to mock me after; you should not have mocked me before; but come your ways.

ROSALIND. Now, Hercules be thy speed, young man!

CELIA. I would I were invisible, to catch the strong fellow by the leg.

[CHARLES *and* ORLANDO *wrestle.*]

ROSALIND. O excellent young man!

CELIA. If I had a thunderbolt in mine eye, I can tell who should down.

[CHARLES *is thrown. Shout.*]

---

[47] *Misprised* is *prised amiss*, that is, *undervalued*. So, in the first scene, Oliver, muttering to himself of his brother's virtues and popularity, shows his envy by saying, "I am altogether *misprised.*"

[48] *To deny* is another gerundial infinitive, and so is equivalent to *in denying.* See page 6, note 22.

[49] Never *in grace*, or *in favour*; never looked upon favourably.

DUKE FREDERICK. No more, no more.
ORLANDO. Yes, I beseech your grace; I am not yet well breathed.[50]
DUKE FREDERICK. How dost thou, Charles?
LE BEAU. He cannot speak, my lord.
DUKE FREDERICK. Bear him away.—[CHARLES *is borne out.*]
What is thy name, young man?
ORLANDO. Orlando, my liege; the youngest son of Sir Rowland de
Bois.
DUKE FREDERICK. I would thou hadst been son to some man else.
The world esteem'd thy father honourable,
But I did find him still mine enemy:
Thou shouldst[51] have better pleas'd me with this deed
Hadst thou descended from another house.
But fare thee well; thou art a gallant youth;
I would thou hadst told me of another father.

[*Exeunt* DUKE FREDERICK, *Train, and* LE BEAU.]

CELIA. Were I my father, coz, would I do this?
ORLANDO. I am more proud to be Sir Rowland's son,
His youngest son;—and would not change that calling
To be adopted heir to Frederick.
ROSALIND. My father loved Sir Rowland as his soul,
And all the world was of my father's mind:
Had I before known this young man his son,
I should have given him tears unto entreaties,[52]
Ere he should thus have ventur'd.
CELIA. Gentle cousin,
Let us go thank him, and encourage him:
My father's rough and envious[53] disposition
Sticks me at heart.—Sir, you have well deserv'd:
If you do keep your promises in love
But justly, as you have exceeded promise,
Your mistress shall be happy.
ROSALIND. Gentleman,

---

[50] *Well breathed* is *well exercised.* Orlando means that he is not yet fairly warm with his work. The verb *to breathe* often occurs in this sense.

[51] *Shouldst* in the sense of *wouldst.* The auxiliaries *could, should,* and *would* in Shakespeare's time were used interchangeably, and he has many instances of such use. In Rosalind's second speech below, we have it again: "That *could* give more"; *could* for *would.*

[52] Would have given him tears *in addition* to entreaties.

[53] In the Poet's time, *envy* and *envious* were generally used for *malice* and *malicious.* So in the English Bible.

[*Giving him a chain from her neck.*]

Wear this for me; one out of suits[54] with fortune,
That could give more, but that her hand lacks means.—
Shall we go, coz!
CELIA. Ay.—Fare you well, fair gentleman.
ORLANDO. Can I not say, I thank you? My better parts
Are all thrown down; and that which here stands up
Is but a quintain,[55] a mere lifeless block.
ROSALIND. He calls us back:[56] my pride fell with my fortunes:
I'll ask him what he would.—Did you call, sir?
Sir, you have wrestled well, and overthrown
More than your enemies.
CELIA. Will you go, coz?
ROSALIND. Have with you—Fare you well.

[*Exeunt* ROSALIND *and* CELIA.]

ORLANDO. What passion hangs these weights upon my tongue?
I cannot speak to her, yet she urged conference.
O poor Orlando! thou art overthrown!
Or Charles, or something weaker, masters thee.

[*Re-enter* LE BEAU.]

LE BEAU. Good sir, I do in friendship counsel you
To leave this place. Albeit you have deserv'd
High commendation, true applause, and love,
Yet such is now the Duke's condition,[57]
That he misconstrues all that you have done.
The Duke is humorous:[58] what he is, indeed,
More suits you to conceive than I to speak of.

---

[54] *Out of suits* is *out of favour*; thrown off or discarded by fortune.

[55] A *quintain* was a figure set up for tilters to run at, in a mock tournament. The form was a post with a cross-bar fixed to the top, turning on a pivot, having a broad board at one end, and a bag full of sand at the other. In the sport, if the figure were struck on the shield, the quintain turned on its pivot and hit the assailant with the sand bag. The skill consisted in striking the quintain dexterously so as to avoid the blow. Orlando is talking to himself in this speech, the ladies having withdrawn.

[56] Orlando has not called them back: why, then, does Rosalind say this? Perhaps she wants to talk further with him.

[57] This word occurs very often in the sense of *temper* or *disposition*. So, in *The Merchant*, i. 2, Portia says of the Moorish Prince, who comes to woo her, "If he have the *condition* of a. saint, and the complexion of a devil, I had rather he should shrive me than wive me."

[58] *Humorous* here is *capricious, moody, crotchety*, or *going by fits and starts*. A frequent usage.

ORLANDO. I thank you, sir: and pray you tell me this,—
   Which of the two was daughter of the Duke
   That here was at the wrestling?
LE BEAU. Neither his daughter, if we judge by manners;
   But yet, indeed, the smaller is his daughter:
   The other is daughter to the banish'd Duke,
   And here detain'd by her usurping uncle,
   To keep his daughter company; whose loves
   Are dearer than the natural bond of sisters.
   But I can tell you that of late this Duke
   Hath ta'en displeasure 'gainst his gentle niece,
   Grounded upon no other argument
   But that the people praise her for her virtues
   And pity her for her good father's sake;
   And, on my life, his malice 'gainst the lady
   Will suddenly break forth. Sir, fare you well!
   Hereafter, in a better world than this,[59]
   I shall desire more love and knowledge of you.
ORLANDO. I rest much bounden to you: fare you well.—

   [*Exit* LE BEAU.]

   Thus must I from the smoke into the smother;[60]
   From tyrant Duke unto a tyrant brother:—
   But Heavenly Rosalind! [*Exit.*]

SCENE III.

A Room in the Palace.

[*Enter* CELIA *and* ROSALIND.]

CELIA. Why, cousin; why, Rosalind;—Cupid have mercy!—Not a
   word?
ROSALIND. Not one to throw at a dog.
CELIA. No, thy words are too precious to be cast away upon curs,
   throw some of them at me; come, lame me with reasons.
ROSALIND. Then there were two cousins laid up; when the one
   should be lamed with reasons and the other mad without any.
CELIA. But is all this for your father?
ROSALIND. No, some of it is for my child's father. O, how full of
   briers is this working-day world!

---

[59] Probably meaning "in a better state of things than the present."
[60] That is, from *bad to worse*. A proverbial phrase, apparently.

CELIA. They are but burs, cousin, thrown upon thee in holiday foolery; if we walk not in the trodden paths, our very petticoats will catch them.

ROSALIND. I could shake them off my coat: these burs are in my heart.

CELIA. Hem them away.

ROSALIND. I would try, if I could cry *hem* and have him.

CELIA. Come, come, wrestle with thy affections.

ROSALIND. O, they take the part of a better wrestler than myself.

CELIA. O, a good wish upon you! you will try in time, in despite of a fall.[61] But, turning these jests out of service, let us talk in good earnest: is it possible, on such a sudden, you should fall into so strong a liking with old Sir Rowland's youngest son?

ROSALIND. The Duke my father loved his father dearly.

CELIA. Doth it therefore ensue that you should love his son dearly? By this kind of chase I should hate him, for my father hated his father dearly;[62] yet I hate not Orlando.

ROSALIND. No, 'faith, hate him not, for my sake.

CELIA. Why should I not? doth he not deserve well?[63]

ROSALIND. Let me love him for that; and do you love him because I do.—Look, here comes the Duke.

CELIA. With his eyes full of anger.

[*Enter* DUKE FREDERICK, *with* Lords.]

DUKE FREDERICK. Mistress, dispatch you with your safest haste,
And get you from our court.

ROSALIND. Me, uncle?

DUKE FREDERICK. You, cousin:
Within these ten days if that thou be'st found
So near our public court as twenty miles,
Thou diest for it.

ROSALIND. I do beseech your grace,
Let me the knowledge of my fault bear with me:
If with myself I hold intelligence,
Or have acquaintance with mine own desires;
If that I do not dream, or be not frantic,—

---

[61] A quibble is probably intended between *falling* in love and *falling* by a wrestler's hand.

[62] In Shakespeare's time, it was just as correct to speak of *hating* dearly as of loving dearly; of a dear *foe* as of a dear friend. So in *Hamlet*, i. 2: "Would I had met my *dearest foe* in Heaven, or ever I had seen that day."

[63] Celia here speaks ironically, her meaning apparently being, "It was because your father deserved well that my father hated him; and ought I not, by your reasoning, to hate Orlando for the same cause?"

As I do trust I am not,—then, dear uncle,
Never so much as in a thought unborn
Did I offend your highness.
DUKE FREDERICK. Thus do all traitors;
If their purgation[64] did consist in words,
They are as innocent as grace itself:—
Let it suffice thee that I trust thee not.
ROSALIND. Yet your mistrust cannot make me a traitor:
Tell me whereon the likelihood depends.
DUKE FREDERICK. Thou art thy father's daughter; there's enough.
ROSALIND. So was I when your highness took his dukedom;
So was I when your highness banish'd him:
Treason is not inherited, my lord:
Or, if we did derive it from our friends,
What's that to me? my father was no traitor!
Then, good my liege, mistake me not so much
To think my poverty is treacherous.
CELIA. Dear sovereign, hear me speak.
DUKE FREDERICK. Ay, Celia: we stay'd her for your sake,
Else had she with her father rang'd along.
CELIA. I did not then entreat to have her stay;
It was your pleasure, and your own remorse:[65]
I was too young that time to value her;
But now I know her: if she be a traitor,
Why so am I: we still have slept together,
Rose at an instant, learn'd, play'd, eat together;
And wheresoe'er we went, like Juno's swans,
Still we went coupled and inseparable.
DUKE FREDERICK. She is too subtle for thee; and her smoothness,
Her very silence, and her patience
Speak to the people, and they pity her.
Thou art a Fool: she robs thee of thy name;
And thou wilt show more bright and seem more virtuous
When she is gone: then open not thy lips;
Firm and irrevocable is my doom
Which I have pass'd upon her: she is banish'd.
CELIA. Pronounce that sentence, then, on me, my liege:
I cannot live out of her company.
DUKE FREDERICK. You are a Fool.—You, niece, provide yourself:
If you outstay the time, upon mine honour,
And in the greatness of my word, you die.

---

[64] *Purgation* is *proof of innocence*; clearing themselves of the matter charged.
[65] *Remorse*, as usual, for *pity* or *compassion*.

[*Exeunt* DUKE FREDERICK *and* Lords.]

CELIA. O my poor Rosalind! whither wilt thou go?
  Wilt thou change fathers? I will give thee mine.
  I charge thee be not thou more griev'd than I am.
ROSALIND. I have more cause.
CELIA. Thou hast not, cousin;
  Pr'ythee be cheerful: know'st thou not the Duke
  Hath banish'd me, his daughter?
ROSALIND. That he hath not.
CELIA. No! hath not? Rosalind lacks, then, the love
  Which teacheth thee that thou and I am one:
  Shall we be sund'red? shall we part, sweet girl?
  No; let my father seek another heir.
  Therefore devise with me how we may fly,
  Whither to go, and what to bear with us:
  And do not seek to take your charge upon you,
  To bear your griefs yourself, and leave me out;
  For, by this Heaven, now at our sorrows pale,
  Say what thou canst, I'll go along with thee.
ROSALIND. Why, whither shall we go?
CELIA. To seek my uncle in the Forest of Arden.
ROSALIND. Alas! what danger will it be to us,
  Maids as we are, to travel forth so far?
  Beauty provoketh thieves sooner than gold.
CELIA. I'll put myself in poor and mean attire,
  And with a kind of umber[66] smirch my face;
  The like do you; so shall we pass along,
  And never stir assailants.
ROSALIND. Were it not better,
  Because that I am more than common tall,
  That I did suit me all points like a man?
  A gallant curtle-axe[67] upon my thigh,
  A boar spear in my hand; and,—in my heart
  Lie there what hidden woman's fear there will[68]—
  We'll have a swashing[69] and a martial outside,
  As many other mannish cowards have

---

[66] *Umber* was a dusky, yellow-coloured earth, from Umbria in Italy.
  [67] This was one of the old words for a *cutlass*, or short, crooked sword. It was variously spelt, *courtlas, courtlax, curtlax.*
  [68] That is, "Whatever hidden woman's fear lies in my heart."
  [69] *Swashing* is *dashing, swaggering.* So in Fuller's *Worthies of England*: "A ruffian is the same with a swaggerer, so called, because endeavouring to make that side swag or weigh down, whereon he engageth. The same also with *swash-buckler*, from swashing or making a noise on bucklers."

That do outface it with their semblances.
CELIA. What shall I call thee when thou art a man?
ROSALIND. I'll have no worse a name than Jove's own page,
    And, therefore, look you call me Ganymede.
    But what will you be call'd?
CELIA. Something that hath a reference to my state:
    No longer Celia, but Aliena.
ROSALIND. But, cousin, what if we essay'd to steal
    The clownish Fool out of your father's court?
    Would he not be a comfort to our travel?
CELIA. He'll go along o'er the wide world with me;
    Leave me alone to woo him. Let's away,
    And get our jewels and our wealth together;
    Devise the fittest time and safest way
    To hide us from pursuit that will be made
    After my flight. Now go we in content
    To liberty, and not to banishment. [*Exeunt.*]

ACT II.

SCENE I.

The Forest of Arden.

[*Enter* DUKE SENIOR, AMIENS, *and other* Lords, *in the dress of Foresters.*]

DUKE SENIOR. Now, my co-mates and brothers in exile,
    Hath not old custom made this life more sweet
    Than that of painted pomp? Are not these woods
    More free from peril than the envious Court?
    Here feel we not the penalty of Adam.[70]
    The seasons' difference: as the icy fang
    And churlish chiding of the winter's wind,—
    Which when it[71] bites and blows upon my body,
    Even till I shrink with cold, I smile and say,
    This is no flattery,—these are counsellors
    That feelingly persuade me what I am."
    Sweet are the uses of adversity;

---

[70] The curse, or *penalty*, denounced upon Adam was, "In the sweat of thy face shalt thou eat bread." This is what the Duke and his co-mates do *not* feel: "they fleet the time *carelessly*, as they did in the golden world." The Duke then goes on, consistently, to say what they *do* feel.

[71] The using of both the relative and the personal pronouns, in relative clauses, as *which* and *it* in this passage, was not uncommon with the best writers.

Which, like the toad, ugly and venomous,
Wears yet a precious jewel in his head:[72]
And this our life, exempt from public haunt,
Finds tongues in trees, books in the running brooks,
Sermons in stones, and good in everything.
I would not change it.
AMIENS. Happy is your grace,
That can translate the stubbornness of fortune
Into so quiet and so sweet a style.
DUKE SENIOR. Come, shall we go and kill us venison?
And yet it irks me,[73] the poor dappled fools,
Being native burghers of this desert city,
Should, in their own confines, with forked heads,[74]
Have their round haunches gor'd.
FIRST LORD. Indeed, my lord,
The melancholy Jaques grieves at that;
And, in that kind, swears you do more usurp
Than doth your brother that hath banish'd you.
To-day my lord of Amiens and myself
Did steal behind him as he lay along
Under an oak, whose antique root peeps out
Upon the brook that brawls along this wood:
To the which place a poor sequester'd stag,
That from the hunter's aim had ta'en a hurt,
Did come to languish; and, indeed, my lord,

---

[72] The real toadstone, as known to the ancients, was apparently so called from its resemblance to the toad or frog in colour. Pliny says, (trans. Holland,) "The same Coptos sendeth other stones unto us besides, to wit, those which be called Batrachitae; the one like in colour to a frog, a second unto ivory, the third is of a blackish red." Besides this slight reference to the Batrachites, says Mr. King in his *Natural History of Gems and Decorative Stones*, "No further notice of this stone can be traced in the other writers of antiquity. But this singular epithet, primarily intended only to denote the peculiar colour of the stone, furnished later times with the foundation for a most marvellous fable, which long obtained, as the number of examples still preserved attest, universal credit throughout Europe. Understanding the ancient term as implying the natural production of the animal according to the analogy of other similar names, as the Saurites, Echites, &c., doctors taught that the 'toad, ugly and venomous, wears yet a precious jewel in his head.'"—WILLIAM ALDIS WRIGHT.

[73] The verb *to irk* is now seldom used, but its sense in the adjective *irksome* is common. To *irk* is to *grieve, vex,* or *annoy.*

[74] Some question has been made as to what these were. Roger Ascham, in his *Toxophilus*, appears to settle the matter; describing two kinds of arrow-heads as follows: "The one having two points or barbs, looking backward to the steel and feathers, which surely we call in English a broad arrow-head or a swallow-tail; the other having two points stretching forward, and this Englishmen do call a forkhead." And again: "Commodus the Emperor used forked heads, whose fashion Herodian doth lively and naturally describe, saying that they were like the shape of a new moon, wherewith he would smite off the head of a bird, and never miss."

The wretched animal heav'd forth such groans,
That their discharge did stretch his leathern coat
Almost to bursting; and the big round tears
Cours'd one another down his innocent nose
In piteous chase: and thus the hairy Fool,
Much markèd of the melancholy Jaques,
Stood on th' extremest verge of the swift brook,
Augmenting it with tears.[75]
DUKE SENIOR. But what said Jaques?
    Did he not moralize this spectacle?
FIRST LORD. O, yes, into a thousand similes.
    First, for his weeping into the needless[76] stream;
    Poor deer, quoth he *thou mak'st a testament*
    As worldlings do, giving thy sum of more
    To that which had too much: then, being there alone,
    Left and abandoned of his velvet friends;
    'Tis right, quoth he; *thus misery doth part*
    The flux of company: anon, a careless herd,
    Full of the pasture, jumps along by him
    And never stays to greet him; *Ay*, quoth Jaques,
    Sweep on, you fat and greasy citizens;
    'Tis just the fashion; wherefore do you look
    Upon that poor and broken bankrupt there?
    Thus most invectively he pierceth through
    The body of the country, city, court,
    Yea, and of this our life: swearing that we
    Are mere usurpers, tyrants, and what's[77] worse,
    To fright the animals, and to kill them up,[78]
    In their assign'd and native dwelling-place.
DUKE SENIOR. And did you leave him in this contemplation?
SECOND LORD. We did, my lord, weeping and commenting
    Upon the sobbing deer.
DUKE SENIOR. Show me the place:
    I love to cope him in these sullen fits,
    For then he's full of matter.

---

[75] Drayton in the thirteenth song of his *Poly-Olbion* has a fine description of a deer-hunt, which he winds up thus:

> He who the mourner is to his own dying corse,
> Upon the ruthless earth his precious tears lets fall.

And in a note upon the passage he adds, "The hart weepeth at his dying: his tears are held precious in medicine."

[76] *Needless* for *not needing.* Shakespeare abounds in similar language.

[77] *What* for the indefinite pronoun *whatever.* A frequent usage.

[78] "Kill them *up*" is old language for "kill them *off*," or *kill them.*

FIRST LORD. I'll bring you to him straight. [*Exeunt.*]

SCENE II.

A Room in the Palace.

[*Enter* DUKE FREDERICK, Lords, *and* Attendants.]

DUKE FREDERICK. Can it be possible that no man saw them?
 It cannot be: some villains of my court
 Are of consent and sufferance in this.
FIRST LORD. I cannot hear of any that did see her.
 The ladies, her attendants of her chamber,
 Saw her a-bed; and in the morning early
 They found the bed untreasur'd of their mistress.
SECOND LORD. My lord, the roynish[79] clown, at whom so oft
 Your grace was wont to laugh, is also missing.
 Hesperia, the princess' gentlewoman,
 Confesses that she secretly o'erheard
 Your daughter and her cousin much commend
 The parts and graces of the wrestler
 That did but lately foil the sinewy Charles;
 And she believes, wherever they are gone,
 That youth is surely in their company.
DUKE FREDERICK. Send to his brother; fetch that gallant hither:
 If he be absent, bring his brother to me,
 I'll make him find him: do this suddenly;
 And let not search and inquisition quail[80]
 To bring again these foolish runaways. [*Exeunt.*]

SCENE III.

Before OLIVER'*s House.*

[*Enter* ORLANDO *and* ADAM, *meeting.*]

ORLANDO. Who's there?
ADAM. What, my young master? O my gentle master!
 O my sweet master! O you memory[81]

---

[79] *Roynish* properly means *mangy* or *scurvy*. From the French *ronger*, to knaw, eat, or corrode. Used here as a general term of reproach.

[80] To *quail* is to *grow faint*, to *slacken*, *give over.—Inquisition* is *inquiry*, *investigation.*

[81] *Memory* for *memorial* or *remembrancer*. A frequent usage. So in the Communion Service of the Episcopal Church: "A perpetual *memory* of that his precious death," &c.

Of old Sir Rowland! why, what make you here?[82]
Why are you virtuous? why do people love you?
And wherefore are you gentle, strong, and valiant?
Why would you be so fond to overcome
The bonny prizer of the humorous Duke?[83]
Your praise is come too swiftly home before you.
Know you not, master, to some kind of men
Their graces serve them but as enemies?
No more do yours; your virtues, gentle master,
Are sanctified and holy traitors to you.[84]
O, what a world is this, when what is comely
Envenoms him that bears it!

ORLANDO. Why, what's the matter?

ADAM. O unhappy youth,
Come not within these doors; within this roof[85]
The enemy of all your graces lives:
Your brother,—(no, no brother; yet the son—
Yet not the son; I will not call him son—
Of him I was about to call his father)—
Hath heard your praises; and this night he means
To burn the lodging where you use to lie,
And you within it: if he fail of that,
He will have other means to cut you off;
I overheard him and his practices.
This is no place;[86] this house is but a butchery:
Abhor it, fear it, do not enter it.

ORLANDO. Why, whither, Adam, wouldst thou have me go?

ADAM. No matter whither, so you come not here.

ORLANDO. What, wouldst thou have me go and beg my food?
Or with a base and boisterous sword enforce
A thievish living on the common road?
This I must do, or know not what to do:
Yet this I will not do, do how I can:

---

[82] "What *are* you *doing* here?" See page 4, note 13.

[83] "Why would you be so *foolish* as to overcome?" Such was the more common meaning of *fond* in the Poet's time. And he often omits *as* in such cases.—*Priser* is *prize-fighter*, or contender for prizes. Here, as before, humorous has the sense of *moody* or *capricious*. See page 13, note 58.

[84] The Poet is fond of thus mixing incongruous words, in order to express certain complexities of thought. In like sort, even so grave a writer as Richard Hooker has the expression *heavenly fraud*, in a thoroughly good sense.—*Envenoms*, second line after, means *poisons*; not that which makes a. man venomous, but that which acts like venom upon him.

[85] *Roof* for *house*; the common figure of putting a part for the whole.

[86] *Place* here means *residence* or *home*; sometimes used so still.—*Practices*, line before, is *plottings, treacherous devices*.

I rather will subject me to the malice
Of a diverted blood[87] and bloody brother.
ADAM. But do not so. I have five hundred crowns,
The thrifty hire I sav'd under your father,
Which I did store to be my foster-nurse,
When service should in my old limbs lie lame,
And unregarded age in corners thrown;
Take that: and He that doth the ravens feed,
Yea, providently caters for the sparrow,
Be comfort to my age! Here is the gold;
All this I give you. Let me be your servant;
Though I look old, yet I am strong and lusty:
For in my youth I never did apply
Hot and rebellious liquors in my blood;
Nor did not with unbashful forehead woo
The means of weakness and debility;
Therefore my age is as a lusty winter,
Frosty, but kindly.[88] Let me go with you;
I'll do the service of a younger man
In all your business and necessities.
ORLANDO. O good old man; how well in thee appears
The constant service of the antique world,
When service sweat for duty, not for meed!
Thou art not for the fashion of these times,
Where none will sweat but for promotion;
And having that, do choke their service up
Even with the having:[89] it is not so with thee.
But, poor old man, thou prun'st a rotten tree,
That cannot so much as a blossom yield
In lieu of[90] all thy pains and husbandry:
But come thy ways, we'll go along together;
And ere we have thy youthful wages spent
We'll light upon some settled low content.
ADAM. Master, go on; and I will follow thee
To the last gasp, with truth and loyalty.—
From seventeen years till now almost fourscore
Here lived I, but now live here no more.
At seventeen years many their fortunes seek;
But at fourscore it is too late a week:[91]
Yet fortune cannot recompense me better

---

[87] Blood *turned out of its natural course*. Blood here stands for *affection*.
[88] *Kindly* in the sense of *natural*, and therefore *healthy*.
[89] Because their promotion makes them too proud to serve.
[90] In *return for*; as always in Shakespeare.
[91] A *week* put for an indefinite period.

Than to die well and not my master's debtor. [*Exeunt.*]

SCENE IV.

The Forest of Arden.

[*Enter* ROSALIND *in boy's clothes,* CELIA *drest like a Shepherdess, and* TOUCHSTONE.]

ROSALIND. O Jupiter, how weary are my spirits!

TOUCHSTONE. I care not for my spirits, if my legs were not weary.

ROSALIND. I could find in my heart to disgrace my man's apparel, and to cry like a woman; but I must comfort the weaker vessel, as doublet and hose ought to show itself courageous to petticoat; therefore, courage, good Aliena.

CELIA. I pray you bear with me; I can go no further.

TOUCHSTONE. For my part, I had rather bear with you than bear you: yet I should bear no cross,[92] if I did bear you; for I think you have no money in your purse.

ROSALIND. Well, this is the forest of Arden.

TOUCHSTONE. Ay, now am I in Arden: the more Fool I; when I was at home I was in a better place; but travellers must be content.

ROSALIND. Ay, be so, good Touchstone. Look you, who comes here? a young man and an old in solemn[93] talk.

[*Enter* CORIN *and* SILVIUS.]

CORIN. That is the way to make her scorn you still.

SILVIUS. O Corin, that thou knew'st how I do love her!

CORIN. I partly guess; for I have lov'd ere now.

SILVIUS. No, Corin, being old, thou canst not guess;
    Though in thy youth thou wast as true a lover
    As ever sigh'd upon a midnight pillow:
    But if thy love were ever like to mine,—
    As sure I think did never man love so,—
    How many actions most ridiculous
    Hast thou been drawn to by thy fantasy?

CORIN. Into a thousand that I have forgotten.

SILVIUS. O, thou didst then never love so heartily:
    If thou remember'st not the slightest folly

---

[92] In Shakespeare's time certain English coins had a cross stamped on one side, and hence were called *crosses*. This gave occasion for frequent puns. So Scott, in *Woodstock*, chap. iii.: "No devil so frightful as that which dances in the pocket where there is no *cross* to keep him out."

[93] In old language, *solemn* is often used in the sense of *serious* or *earnest*.

That ever love did make thee run into,
Thou hast not lov'd:
Or if thou hast not sat as I do now,
Wearing thy hearer in thy mistress' praise,
Thou hast not lov'd:
Or if thou hast not broke from company
Abruptly, as my passion now makes me,
Thou hast not lov'd.—O Phebe, Phebe, Phebe! [*Exit.*]

ROSALIND. Alas, poor shepherd! searching of thy wound,
I have by hard adventure found mine own.
TOUCHSTONE. And I mine. I remember, when I was in love, I broke
my sword upon a stone, and bid him[94] take that for coming a-night
to Jane Smile: and I remember the kissing of her batlet,[95] and the
cow's dugs that her pretty chapp'd hands had milk'd: and I
remember the wooing of a peascod[96] instead of her; from whom I
took two cods, and giving her them again, said with weeping tears,
Wear these for my sake. We that are true lovers run into strange
capers; but as all is mortal in nature, so is all nature in love
mortal[97] in folly.
ROSALIND. Thou speak'st wiser than thou art 'ware of.
TOUCHSTONE. Nay, I shall ne'er be 'ware of mine own wit till I
break my shins against it.
ROSALIND. Jove, Jove! this shepherd's passion
Is much upon my fashion.
TOUCHSTONE. And mine: but it grows something stale with me.
CELIA. I pray you, one of you question yond man
If he for gold will give us any food:
I faint almost to death.
TOUCHSTONE. Holla, you clown!
ROSALIND. Peace, Fool; he's not thy kinsman.
CORIN. Who calls?
TOUCHSTONE. Your betters, sir.
CORIN. Else are they very wretched.
ROSALIND. Peace, I say.—Good even to you, friend.
CORIN. And to you, gentle sir, and to you all.
ROSALIND. I pr'ythee, shepherd, if that love or gold

---

[94] The imaginary rival for whose visits to Jane the stone was held vicariously responsible.

[95] An instrument with which washers beat clothes.

[96] That is, from the peascod as representing his mistress. *Cod* was formerly used for the *shell* of peas, what we now call the *pod*. Pea-pods seem to have been worn sometimes for ornament.

[97] *Mortal* is said to be used in the Craven dialect as a general intensive, or with the sense of *excessive*. So I have often heard such phrases as "*mortal* great" and "*mortal* tall."

Can in this desert[98] place buy entertainment,
Bring us where we may rest ourselves and feed:
Here's a young maid with travel much oppress'd,
And faints for succour.

CORIN. Fair sir, I pity her,
And wish, for her sake more than for mine own,
My fortunes were more able to relieve her:
But I am shepherd to another man,
And do not shear the fleeces that I graze:
My master is of churlish disposition,
And little recks[99] to find the way to Heaven
By doing deeds of hospitality:
Besides, his cote,[100] his flocks, and bounds of feed,
Are now on sale; and at our sheepcote now,
By reason of his absence, there is nothing
That you will feed on; but what is, come see,
And in my voice[101] most welcome shall you be.

ROSALIND. What is he that shall buy his flock and pasture?

CORIN. That young swain that you saw here but erewhile,
That little cares for buying anything.

ROSALIND. I pray thee, if it stand with honesty,
Buy thou the cottage, pasture, and the flock,
And thou shalt have to pay for it of us.

CELIA. And we will mend thy wages. I like this place,
And willingly could waste[102] my time in it.

CORIN. Assuredly the thing is to be sold:
Go with me: if you like, upon report,
The soil, the profit, and this kind of life,
I will your very faithful feeder be,
And buy it with your gold right suddenly. [*Exeunt.*]

---

[98] *Desert* was used of any wild or uninhabited place.

[99] Little *cares*. The sense of *reck* appears in our word *reckless*.

[100] That is, *cot* or *cottage*; the word is still used in its compound form, as *sheepcote* in the next line.

[101] "As far as my voice has the power to bid you welcome."

[102] *Waste* for *pass* or *spend*.

SCENE V.

Another Part of the Forest.

[*Enter* AMIENS, JAQUES, *and others.*]

SONG.

AMIENS.   *Under the greenwood tree,*
Who loves to lie with me,
And turn his merry note
Unto the sweet bird's throat,
Come hither, come hither, come hither:
Here shall he see no enemy
But winter and rough weather.

JAQUES. More, more, I pr'ythee, more.
AMIENS. It will make you melancholy, Monsieur Jaques.
JAQUES. I thank it. More, I pr'ythee, more. I can suck melancholy out of a song, as a weasel sucks eggs. More, I pr'ythee, more.
AMIENS. My voice is ragged; I know I cannot please you.
JAQUES. I do not desire you to please me; I do desire you to sing. Come, more: another stanza. Call you them stanzas?
AMIENS. What you will, Monsieur Jaques.
JAQUES. Nay, I care not for their names; they owe me nothing.[103] Will you sing?
AMIENS. More at your request than to please myself.
JAQUES. Well then, if ever I thank any man, I'll thank you: but that they call compliment is like the encounter of two dog-apes;[104] and when a man thanks me heartily, methinks have given him a penny, and he renders me the beggarly thanks. Come, sing; and you that will not, hold your tongues.
AMIENS. Well, I'll end the song.—Sirs, cover[105] the while; the Duke will drink under this tree.—He hath been all this day to look you.[106]

---

[103] In Latin, *nomina facere* means to enter an account, because not only the sums, but the *names* of the parties, are entered. Cicero uses *nomina facere* for to lend money, and *nomen solvere* for to pay a debt; and in Livy we have *nomen transcribere in alium* for to transfer a debt to another.

[104] *Dog-apes* are dog-faced baboons.

[105] *Cover* refers to the forthcoming banquet, and seems to be an order for setting out and preparing the table. Accordingly, at the close of the scene, we have "his banquet is prepared."

[106] The Poet repeatedly uses *look* thus as a transitive verb; equivalent to *look for*. So in the *The Merry Wives*, iv. 2: "Mistress Page, I will *look* some linen for your head."

JAQUES. And I have been all this day to avoid him. He is too disputable[107] for my company: I think of as many matters as he; but I give Heaven thanks, and make no boast of them. Come, warble, come.

SONG.

ALL.
Who doth ambition shun,
And loves to live i' the sun,
Seeking the food he eats,
And pleas'd with what he gets,
Come hither, come hither, come hither.
Here shall he see no enemy
But winter and rough weather.

JAQUES. I'll give you a verse to this note that I made yesterday in despite of my invention.[108]
AMIENS. And I'll sing it.
JAQUES. Thus it goes:

If it do come to pass
That any man turn ass,
Leaving his wealth and ease
A stubborn will to please,
Ducdame, ducdame, ducdame;[109]
Here shall he see gross fools as he,
An if he will come to me.

AMIENS. What's that *ducdame?*
JAQUES. 'Tis a Greek invocation,[110] to call fools into a circle. I'll go sleep, if I can; if I cannot, I'll rail against all the first-born of Egypt.[111]
AMIENS. And I'll go seek the Duke; his banquet is prepared.

---

[107] *Disputable* for *disputatious;* according to the indifferent use of active and passive forms then so common.

[108] *Note* is here put for *tune.*—"In despite of my invention" probably means "in despite of my *lack* of invention." Such elliptical expressions are not uncommon in Shakespeare. So in iii. 2, of this play: "He that hath learned no wit by nature nor art may complain of good breeding"; which evidently means "may complain of *want of* good breeding."

[109] *Ducadme* is three Latin words, *duc ad me,* compressed into one, and means *bring him to me.*

[110] The invocation is Latin, not Greek. Of course the Poet knew this. Perhaps Mr. White explains it rightly: "That the cynical Jaques should pass off his Latin for Greek upon Amiens, is but in character."

[111] A proverbial expression for *high-born* persons.

[*Exeunt severally.*]

SCENE VI.

Another part of the Forest.

[*Enter* ORLANDO *and* ADAM.]

ADAM. Dear master, I can go no further: O, I die for food! Here lie I down, and measure out my grave. Farewell, kind master.

ORLANDO. Why, how now, Adam! no greater heart in thee? Live a little; comfort a little; cheer thyself a little. If this uncouth[112] forest yield anything savage, I will either be food for it or bring it for food to thee. Thy conceit[113] is nearer death than thy powers. For my sake be comfortable;[114] hold death awhile at the arm's end: I will here be with thee presently; and if I bring thee not something to eat, I'll give thee leave to die: but if thou diest before I come, thou art a mocker of my labour. Well said![115] thou look'st cheerily: and I'll be with thee quickly.—Yet thou liest in the bleak air: come, I will bear thee to some shelter; and thou shalt not die for lack of a dinner if there live anything in this desert. Cheerily, good Adam! [*Exeunt.*]

SCENE VII.

The Same as in Scene V.

[*A Table set out.* ENTER DUKE SENIOR, AMIENS, *others.*]

DUKE SENIOR. I think he be transform'd into a beast;
For I can nowhere find him like a man.

FIRST LORD. My lord, he is but even now gone hence;
Here was he merry, hearing of a song.

DUKE SENIOR. If he, compact of jars,[116] grow musical,
We shall have shortly discord in the spheres.[117]
Go, seek him; tell him I would speak with him.

---

[112] *Uncouth* properly means *unknown*; hence *strange, wild,* or *savage.*

[113] *Conceit,* as usual, for *conception, thought,* or *apprehension.*

[114] Be *comfortable* for be *comforted,* or *take comfort.* The Poet has many like instances of the endings *-able* and *-ed* used indiscriminately.

[115] *Well said* was a. common colloquial phrase for *well done.*

[116] *Composed* or *made up* of *discords.*

[117] If things are going so contrary to their natural order, the music of the spheres will soon be untuned.

FIRST LORD. He saves my labour by his own approach.

[*Enter* JAQUES.]

DUKE SENIOR. Why, how now, monsieur! what a life is this,
    That your poor friends must woo your company?
    What! you look merrily!
JAQUES. A Fool, a Fool!—I met a Fool i' the forest,
    A motley Fool;[118]—a miserable world!—
    As I do live by food, I met a Fool,
    Who laid him down and bask'd him in the sun,
    And rail'd on Lady Fortune in good terms,
    In good set terms,—and yet a motley Fool.
    Good morrow, Fool, quoth I: *No, sir,* quoth he,
    Call me not Fool till Heaven hath sent me fortune.[119]
    And then he drew a dial from his poke,[120]
    And, looking on it with lack-lustre eye,
    Says very wisely, *It is ten o'clock*:
    Thus we may see, quoth he, *how the world wags*;
    'Tis but an hour ago since it was nine;
    And after one hour more 'twill be eleven;
    And so, from hour to hour, we ripe and ripe,
    And then, from hour to hour, we rot and rot;
    And thereby hangs a tale. When I did hear
    The motley Fool thus moral on the time,
    My lungs began to crow like chanticleer,
    That fools should be so deep contemplative;
    And I did laugh sans intermission
    An hour by his dial.—O noble Fool!
    A worthy Fool!—Motley's the only wear.
DUKE SENIOR. What Fool is this?
JAQUES. O worthy Fool!—One that hath been a courtier,
    And says, if ladies be but young and fair,
    They have the gift to know it: and in his brain,—
    Which is as dry as the remainder biscuit[121]

---

[118] So called because the professional Fool wore a patch-work or parti-coloured dress. The old sense of *motley* still lives in *mottled.*

[119] "It will be time enough to call me rich, when I shall have got rich." So in Ray's *Collection of English Proverbs*: "Fortune favours fools, or fools have the best luck." And Ben Jonson in the Prologue to *The Alchemist*: "Fortune, that favours fools, these two short hours we wish away."

[120] *Poke* is *pocket* or *pouch.*—The Poet repeatedly uses *dial* for what we call a *watch*, as here; also sometimes for *clock.*

[121] So Ben Jonson in the Induction to *Every Man out of his Humour*: "And now and then breaks a *dry biscuit jest*, which, that it may more easily be chew'd, he steeps in his own laughter." And Batman upon Bartholome has the following, quoted by Mr. Wright:

After a voyage,—he hath strange places cramm'd
With observation, the which he vents
In mangled forms.—O that I were a Fool!
I am ambitious for a motley coat.
DUKE SENIOR. Thou shalt have one.
JAQUES. It is my only suit;[122]
Provided that you weed your better judgments
Of all opinion that grows rank in them
That I am wise. I must have liberty
Withal, as large a charter as the wind,[123]
To blow on whom I please; for so fools have:
And they that are most gallèd with my folly,
They most must laugh. And why, sir, must they so?
The "why" is plain as way to parish church:
He that a Fool doth very wisely hit
Doth very foolishly, although he smart,
Not to seem senseless of the bob:[124] if not,
The wise man's folly is anatomiz'd
Even by the squandering glances[125] of the Fool.
Invest me in my motley; give me leave
To speak my mind, and I will through and through
Cleanse the foul body of the infected world,
If they will patiently receive my medicine.
DUKE SENIOR. Fie on thee! I can tell what thou wouldst do.
JAQUES. What, for a counter,[126] would I do but good?
DUKE SENIOR. Most mischievous foul sin, in chiding sin;
For thou thyself hast been a libertine,
As sensual as the brutish sting itself;
And all the embossèd[127] sores and headed evils
That thou with license of free foot hast caught
Wouldst thou disgorge into the general world.

"Good disposition of the brain and evil is known by his deeds, for if the substance of the brain be soft, thin, and clear, it receiveth lightly the feeling and printing of shapes, and likenesses of things. He that hath such a brain is swift, and good of perseverance and teaching. When it is contrary, the brain is not soft: he that hath such a brain receiveth slowly the feeling and printing of things: but nevertheless, when he hath taken and received them, he keepeth them long in mind. And that is sign and token of dryness," &c.

[122] A quibble, of course, between *petition* and *dress*.

[123] "The wind bloweth where it listeth." *Charter* was often used for *liberty*; perhaps from the effect of *Magna Charta* in guarding English freedom.

[124] *Bob* is *blow*, *thrust*, or *hit*.

[125] *Squandering glances* are *random* or *scattering thrusts* or *shots*.

[126] About the time when this play was written, the French *counters*, pieces of false money used in reckoning, were brought into use in England.

[127] *Embossed* is *protuberant*, or *come to a head*, like boils and carbuncles. So, in *King Lear*, ii. 4: "Thou art a boil, a plague sore, an *embossed* carbuncle." The protuberant part of a shield was called the *boss*.

JAQUES. Why, who cries out on pride
  That can therein tax any private party?
  Doth it not flow as hugely as the sea,
  Till that the weary very means do ebb?
  What woman in the city do I name
  When that I say, The city-woman bears
  The cost of princes on unworthy shoulders?
  Who can come in and say that I mean her,
  When such a one as she, such is her neighbour?
  Or what is he of basest function,[128]
  That says his bravery[129] is not on my cost—
  Thinking that I mean him—but therein suits
  His folly to the metal of my speech?
  There then; how then? what then? Let me see wherein
  My tongue hath wrong'd him: if it do him right,
  Then he hath wrong'd himself; if he be free,
  Why then, my taxing like a wild-goose flies,
  Unclaim'd of any man.—But who comes here?

[*Enter* ORLANDO, *with his sword drawn.*]

ORLANDO. Forbear, and eat no more!
JAQUES. Why, I have eat none yet.
ORLANDO. Nor shalt not, till necessity be serv'd.
JAQUES. Of what kind should this cock come of?[130]
DUKE SENIOR. Art thou thus bolden'd, man, by thy distress:
  Or else a rude despiser of good manners,
  That in civility thou seem'st so empty?
ORLANDO. You touch'd my vein at first: the thorny point
  Of bare distress hath ta'en from me the show
  Of smooth civility: yet am I inland bred,
  And know some nurture.[131] But forbear, I say;
  He dies that touches any of this fruit
  Till I and my affairs are answered.

---

[128] Of lowest or meanest *calling* or *occupation*; that is, a *tailor*, or one whose "soul is his clothes."

[129] *Bravery* is fine showy dress or equipage.

[130] This doubling of the preposition was not uncommon in the Poet's time. He has many instances of it. Thus, a little later in this play: "The scene wherein we play *in.*" So, too, in *Coriolanus*, ii. I: "*In* what enormity is Marcius poor *in?*" And in *Romeo and Juliet*, Act i., *Chorus:* "That fair *for* which love groan'd *for.*"

[131] *Nurture* is education, culture, good-breeding. So in Prospero's description of Caliban: "A devil, a born devil, on whose nature *nurture* can never stick."—*Inland*, the commentators say, is here opposed to *upland*. which meant *rude, unbred.* I am apt to think the use of the word grew from the fact, that up to the Poet's time all the main springs of culture and civility in England were literally *inland*, remote from the sea.

JAQUES. An you will not be answered with reason, I must die.
DUKE SENIOR. What would you have? your gentleness shall force
More than your force move us to gentleness.
ORLANDO. I almost die for food, and let me have it.
DUKE SENIOR. Sit down and feed, and welcome to our table.
ORLANDO. Speak you so gently? Pardon me, I pray you:
I thought that all things had been savage here;
And therefore put I on the countenance
Of stern commandment. But whate'er you are
That in this desert inaccessible,
Under the shade of melancholy boughs,
Lose and neglect the creeping hours of time;
If ever you have look'd on better days,
If ever been where bells have knoll'd to church,
If ever sat at any good man's feast,
If ever from your eyelids wip'd a tear,
And know what 'tis to pity and be pitied,—
Let gentleness my strong enforcement be:
In the which hope I blush, and hide my sword.
DUKE SENIOR. True is it that we have seen better days,
And have with holy bell been knoll'd to church,
And sat at good men's feasts, and wip'd our eyes
Of drops that sacred pity hath engender'd:
And therefore sit you down in gentleness,
And take upon command[132] what help we have,
That to your wanting may be minister'd.
ORLANDO. Then but forbear your food a little while,
Whiles, like a doe, I go to find my fawn,
And give it food. There is an old poor man
Who after me hath many a weary step
Limp'd in pure love: till he be first sufficed,—
Oppress'd with two weak evils, age and hunger,—
I will not touch a bit.
DUKE SENIOR. Go find him out.
And we will nothing waste till you return.
ORLANDO. I thank ye; and be blest for your good comfort! [*Exit.*]
DUKE SENIOR. Thou seest we are not all alone unhappy;
This wide and universal theatre
Presents more woeful pageants than the scene
Wherein we play in.
JAQUES. All the world's a stage,

[132] "Take as you may choose to order, at your will and pleasure." In Lodge's tale we have it thus: "Gerismond tooke him by the hand and badde him welcome, willing him to sit downe in his place, and not onely to eat his fill, but *be lord of the feast*."

And all the men and women merely players;
They have their exits and their entrances;
And one man in his time plays many parts,
His acts being seven ages.[133] At first the infant,
Mewling and puking in the nurse's arms;
Then the whining school-boy, with his satchel
And shining morning face, creeping like snail
Unwillingly to school. And then the lover,
Sighing like furnace, with a woeful ballad
Made to his mistress' eyebrow. Then a soldier,
Full of strange oaths, and bearded like the pard,[134] *leopard*
Jealous in honour, sudden and quick in quarrel,
Seeking the bubble reputation
Even in the cannon's mouth. And then the justice,
In fair round belly with good capon lined,
With eyes severe and beard of formal cut,
Full of wise saws and modern instances;[135]
And so he plays his part. The sixth age shifts
Into the lean and slipper'd pantaloon,[136]
With spectacles on nose and pouch on side;
His youthful hose, well saved, a world too wide
For his shrunk shank; and his big manly voice,
Turning again toward childish treble, pipes
And whistles in his[137] sound. Last scene of all,
That ends this strange eventful history,
Is second childishness and mere oblivion;
Sans teeth, sans eyes, sans taste, sans everything.

[*Re-enter* ORLANDO *with* ADAM.]

DUKE SENIOR. Welcome. Set down your venerable burden,

---

[133] *Totus mundus agit histrionem,* an observation occurring in one of the fragments of Petronius, is said to have been the motto over Shakespeare's theatre, the Globe, and was probably a familiar apothegm in his day. The division of human life into certain stages, or epochs, had also a classical origin. In some Greek verses attributed to Solon,— and, whether written by him or not, certainly as old as the middle of the first century,— the life of man is divided into ten ages of seven years each. Other Greek authors distributed it into seven parts, and Varro the Roman into five. A Hebrew doctor of the ninth century, and a Hebrew Poet of the twelfth, have made a similar distribution.

[134] *Pard* is one of the old names for *leopard.*

[135] *Saws* are *sayings;* often so used. *Modern* is *trite, common, familiar.* Men may still be seen overflowing with stale, threadbare proverbs and phrases, and imagining themselves wondrous wise. *Instances,* here, is *examples, illustrations, anecdotes,* such as many an official wiseacre is fond of repeating on all occasions.

[136] The *pantaloon* was a stereotyped character in the old Italian farces: it represented a thin, emaciated old man, in *slippers.*

[137] *His* for *its,* the latter not being then in use.

And let him feed.

ORLANDO. I thank you most for him.

ADAM. So had you need:—
I scarce can speak to thank you for myself.

DUKE SENIOR. Welcome; fall to: I will not trouble you
As yet, to question you about your fortunes.—
Give us some music; and, good cousin, sing.

SONG.

AMIENS.
 Blow, blow, thou winter wind,
  Thou art not so unkind
   As man's ingratitude;
  Thy tooth is not so keen,
  Because thou art not seen,
   Although thy breath be rude.
 Heigh-ho! sing heigh-ho! unto the green holly:
 Most friendship is feigning, most loving mere folly:
  Then, heigh-ho, the holly!
   This life is most jolly.

 Freeze, freeze, thou bitter sky,
  That dost not bite so nigh
   As benefits forgot:
 Though thou the waters warp,[138]
  Thy sting is not so sharp
  As friend remember'd not.
 Heigh-ho! sing heigh-ho! unto the green holly:
 Most friendship is feigning, most loving mere folly:
  Then, heigh-ho, the holly!
   This life is most jolly.

DUKE SENIOR. If that you were the good Sir Rowland's son,—
As you have whisper'd faithfully you were,
And as mine eye doth his effigies witness
Most truly limn'd[139] and living in your face,—
Be truly welcome hither: I am the Duke

---

[138] In the Poet's time the verb *warp* was sometimes used for *weave,*—a sense now retained only in the substantive. Thus in Sternhold's version of the Psalms: "While he doth mischief *warp*," and "Such wicked wiles to *warp*"; where we should say *weave*. In Hickes' *Thesaurus* is found a Saxon proverb, "Winter shall *warp water*." And Propertius has a line containing the same figure: "Africus in glaciem frigore *nectit aquas*." The appropriateness of the figure may be seen in the fine network appearance which water assumes in the first stages of crystallization.

[139] *Limn'd* is *lined*, or *depicted*.—It is hardly needful to say that *effigies* is the same in sense as *image*.

That lov'd your father. The residue of your fortune,
Go to my cave and tell me.—Good old man,
Thou art right welcome as thy master is;
Support him by the arm.—Give me your hand,
And let me all your fortunes understand. [*Exeunt.*]

ACT III.

SCENE I.

A Room in the Palace.

[*Enter* DUKE FREDERICK, OLIVER, LORDS *and* Attendants.]

DUKE FREDERICK. Not see him since? Sir, sir, that cannot be:
    But were I not the better part made mercy,
    I should not seek an absent argument[140]
    Of my revenge, thou present. But look to it:
    Find out thy brother wheresoe'er he is:
    Seek him with candle; bring him dead or living
    Within this twelvemonth, or turn thou no more
    To seek a living in our territory.
    Thy lands, and all things that thou dost call thine
    Worth seizure, do we seize into our hands,
    Till thou canst quit[141] thee by thy brother's mouth
    Of what we think against thee.
OLIVER. O that your highness knew my heart in this!
    I never lov'd my brother in my life.
DUKE FREDERICK. More villain thou.—Well, push him out of
    doors,
    And let my officers of such a nature
    Make an extent[142] upon his house and lands:
    Do this expediently,[143] and turn him going. [*Exeunt.*]

---

[140] *Argument* was used in a good many senses: here it means *object.*

[141] *Quit* here is *acquit.* The Poet has it repeatedly in that sense. So in *Measure for Measure,* v. 1: "Thou'rt condemn'd: but, for those earthly faults, I quit them all." And in *Henry V.,* ii. 1: "God *quit you* in His mercy!"

[142] A law phrase, thus explained by Blackstone: "The process hereon is usually called an *extent* or *extendi facias,* because the Sheriff is to cause the lands, &c., to be appraised to their full *extended* value, before he delivers them to the plaintiff."

[143] *Expediently* for *expeditiously.* So the Poet uses *expedient* for *expeditious.*

SCENE II.

The Forest of Arden.

[*Enter* ORLANDO, *with a paper, which he hangs on a tree.*]

ORLANDO. Hang there, my verse, in witness of my love;
And thou, thrice-crownèd Queen of Night,[144] survey
With thy chaste eye, from thy pale sphere above,
Thy huntress' name, that my full life doth sway.
O Rosalind! these trees shall be my books,
And in their barks my thoughts I'll character,
That every eye which in this forest looks
Shall see thy virtue witness'd every where.
Run, run, Orlando; carve on every tree,
The fair, the chaste, and unexpressive[145] she. [*Exit.*]

[*Enter* CORIN *and* TOUCHSTONE.]

CORIN. And how like you this shepherd's life, Master Touchstone?
TOUCHSTONE. Truly, shepherd, in respect of itself, it is a good life;
but in respect that it is a shepherd's life, it is naught. In respect that
it is solitary, I like it very well; but in respect that it is private, it is
a very vile life. Now in respect it is in the fields, it pleaseth me
well; but in respect it is not in the court, it is tedious. As it is a
spare life, look you, it fits my humour well; but as there is no more
plenty in it, it goes much against my stomach. Hast any philosophy
in thee, shepherd?
CORIN. No more but that I know the more one sickens, the worse at
ease he is; and that he that wants money, means, and content, is
without three good friends; that the property of rain is to wet, and

---

[144] Luna Queen of Night, Proserpine Queen of Hades, and Diana the Goddess of
Chastity, were all three sometimes identified in classical mythology; hence the epithet
thrice-crowned. In Chapman's *Hymns to Night and to Cynthia,* which were doubtless
well known to Shakespeare, we have the following highly poetical passage:

> Nature's bright *eye-sight,* and the night's fair soul,
> That with thy *triple forehead* dost control
> Earth, seas, and hell.

[145] *Inexpressible* she; the active form with the passive sense. So Milton in his *Hymn
on the Nativity*:

> Harping, in loud and solemn quire,
> With *unexpressive* notes, to Heaven's new-born Heir.

fire to burn; that good pasture makes fat sheep; and that a great cause of the night is lack of the sun; that he that hath learned no wit by nature nor art may complain of good breeding,[146] or comes of a very dull kindred.

TOUCHSTONE. Such a one is a natural[147] philosopher. Wast ever in court, shepherd?

CORIN. No, truly.

TOUCHSTONE. Then thou art damned.

CORIN. Nay, I hope,—

TOUCHSTONE. Truly, thou art damned, like an ill-roasted egg, all on one side.

CORIN. For not being at court? Your reason.

TOUCHSTONE. Why, if thou never wast at court, thou never saw'st good manners; if thou never saw'st good manners, then thy manners must be wicked; and wickedness is sin, and sin is damnation. Thou art in a parlous[148] state, shepherd.

CORIN. Not a whit, Touchstone; those that are good manners at the court are as ridiculous in the country as the behaviour of the country is most mockable at the court. You told me you salute not at the court, but you kiss[149] your hands; that courtesy would be uncleanly if courtiers were shepherds.

TOUCHSTONE. Instance, briefly; come, instance.

CORIN. Why, we are still handling our ewes; and their fells,[150] you know, are greasy.

TOUCHSTONE. Why, do not your courtier's hands sweat? and is not the grease of a mutton as wholesome as the sweat of a man? Shallow, shallow: a better instance, I say; come.

CORIN. Besides, our hands are hard.

TOUCHSTONE. Your lips will feel them the sooner. Shallow again. A more sounder[151] instance, come.

CORIN. And they are often tarred over with the surgery of our sheep; and would you have us kiss tar? The courtier's hands are perfumed with civet.

---

[146] In Jonson's *Sad Shepherd*, Lionel says of Amie: "She's sick *of* the young shepherd that bekist her; "sick *for want* of him. The usage occurs repeatedly in Shakespeare. See page 28, note 108.

[147] *Natural* being a common term for a fool, Touchstone puns on the word.

[148] *Parlous* is an old form of *perilous*; sometimes used with a dash of humour, as appears to be the case in this instance.

[149] *But you kiss* here means *without kissing*. The Poet elsewhere uses *but* in this way. So in *Hamlet*, i. 3: "Do not sleep *but* let me hear from you." Here the meaning clearly is, "Do not sleep *without letting* me hear from you."

[150] *Hides* or *skins*; as in Jonson's *Discoveries*: "A prince is the pastor of the people. He ought to shear, not to flea his sheep; to take their fleeces, not their *fells*."

[151] Comparatives, and superlatives too, were thus doubled by all writers and speakers in Shakespeare's time.

TOUCHSTONE. Most shallow man! thou worm's-meat in respect of[152] a good piece of flesh indeed! Learn of the wise, and perpend:[153] Civet is of a baser birth than tar,—the very uncleanly flux of a cat. Mend the instance, shepherd.

CORIN. You have too courtly a wit for me: I'll rest.

TOUCHSTONE. Wilt thou rest damned? God help thee, shallow man! God make incision in thee![154] thou art raw.

CORIN. Sir, I am a true labourer: I earn that I eat, get that I wear, owe no man hate, envy no man's happiness, glad of other men's good, content with my harm; and the greatest of my pride is to see my ewes graze and my lambs suck.

TOUCHSTONE. That is another simple sin in you: to bring the ewes and the rams together, and to offer to get your living by the copulation of cattle; to be bawd to a bell-wether; and to betray a she-lamb of a twelvemonth to crooked-pated, old, cuckoldly ram, out of all reasonable match. If thou be'st not damned for this, the devil himself will have no shepherds; I cannot see else how thou shouldst 'scape.

CORIN. Here comes young Master Ganymede, my new mistress's brother.

[*Enter* ROSALIND, *reading a paper.*]

ROSALIND.   *From the east to western Ind,*
              No jewel is like Rosalind.
              Her worth, being mounted on the wind,
              Through all the world bears Rosalind.
              All the pictures fairest lined[155]
              Are but black to Rosalind.
              Let no face be kept in mind
              But the fair of Rosalind.

TOUCHSTONE. I'll rhyme you so eight years together, dinners, and suppers, and sleeping hours excepted. It is the right butter-women's rate[156] to market.

ROSALIND. Out, Fool!

---

[152] In *respect of* is in *comparison with.* Often so.

[153] *Perpend* is *consider,* or *weigh mentally.*

[154] Alluding, apparently, to the practice of surgeons, who used *cuttings* and burnings for the healing of a disease called the *simples*; a quibble being implied withal between *simples* and *simpleton*. His being *raw* is the reason why incision should be made, in Touchstone's logic. Bear in mind that *raw* is used in the double sense of *green* and *sore,* and perhaps this will render the passage clear enough.

[155] *Lined* is *delineated* or *drawn.*

[156] The *jog-trot pace* of dairy-women going to market is now all out of date, so that we have no chance of witnessing it.

TOUCHSTONE. For a taste:

> If a hart do lack a hind,
> Let him seek out Rosalind.
> If the cat will after kind,
> So be sure will Rosalind.
> Winter garments must be lin'd,
> So must slender Rosalind.
> They that reap must sheaf and bind,—
> Then to cart with Rosalind.
> Sweetest nut hath sourest rind,
> Such a nut is Rosalind.
> He that sweetest rose will find
> Must find love's prick, and Rosalind.

This is the very false gallop[157] of verses: why do you infect yourself with them?

ROSALIND. Peace, you dull Fool! I found them on a tree.

TOUCHSTONE. Truly, the tree yields bad fruit.

ROSALIND. I'll graft it with you, and then I shall graft it with a medlar. Then it will be the earliest fruit[158] i' the country: for you'll be rotten ere you be half ripe, and that's the right virtue of the medlar.

TOUCHSTONE. You have said; but whether wisely or no, let the forest judge.

[*Enter* CELIA, *reading a paper.*]

ROSALIND. Peace!
Here comes my sister, reading: stand aside.

CELIA. [*Reads.*] *Why should this a desert be?*
> *For[159] it is unpeopled? No;*
> *Tongues I'll hang on every tree*
> *That shall civil[160] sayings show:*

---

[157] So in Nashe's *Pierce Pennilesse*, 1593: "I would trot a *false gallop* through the rest of his ragged *verses*, but that, if I should retort the rime doggerel aright, I must make my verses (as he doth) run *hobbling*, like a brewer's cart upon the stones, and observe no measure in their feet."

[158] The medlar is one of the latest fruits, being uneatable till the end of November. Moreover, though the *latest* of fruits to *ripen*, it is one of the *earliest* to rot. Does Rosalind mean that when the tree is graffed with Touchstone, its fruit will rot earlier than ever?

[159] *For* was often used where we should use *because*.

[160] *Civil* is here used in the same sense as when we say, *civil* wisdom and *civil* life, in opposition to a solitary state.

> *Some, how brief the life of man*
> *Runs his erring pilgrimage,*
> *That the stretching of a span*
> *Buckles in his sum of age.*
> *Some, of violated vows*
> *'Twixt the souls of friend and friend;*
> *But upon the fairest boughs,*
> *Or at every sentence end,*
> *Will I Rosalinda write,*
> *Teaching all that read to know*
> *The quintessence of every sprite*
> *Heaven would in little*[161] *show.*
> *Therefore Heaven nature charg'd*
> *That one body should be fill'd*
> *With all graces wide-enlarg'd:*
> *Nature presently distill'd*
> *Helen's cheek, but not her heart;*
> *Cleopatra's majesty;*
> *Atalanta's better part;*[162]
> *Sad Lucretia's modesty.*
> *Thus Rosalind of many parts*
> *By Heavenly synod was devis'd,*
> *Of many faces, eyes, and hearts,*
> *To have the touches*[163] *dearest priz'd.*
> *Heaven would that she these gifts should have,*
> *And I to live and die her slave.*

ROSALIND. O most gentle pulpiter! what tedious homily of love have you wearied your parishioners withal, and never cried, *Have patience, good people!*

CELIA. How now! back, friends:—shepherd, go off a little:—go with him, sirrah.

TOUCHSTONE. Come, shepherd, let us make an honourable retreat; though not with bag and baggage, yet with scrip and scrippage. [*Exeunt* CORIN *and* TOUCHSTONE.]

CELIA. Didst thou hear these verses?

ROSALIND. O, yes, I heard them all, and more too; for some of them

---

[161] *In little* means *in miniature.*

[162] The commentators have been a good deal puzzled to make out what this better part really was. It must have been that wherein Atalanta surpassed the other ladies mentioned. Now she seems to have been the nimblest-footed of all the ancient girls; so fleet, that she ran clean away from all her lovers, till one of them hit upon the device of throwing golden apples in her way. This would infer exquisite symmetry and proportion of form; and Orlando must of course imagine all formal, as well as all mental and moral graces, in his "heavenly Rosalind."

[163] *Touches* is *traits* or *qualities,* or both.

had in them more feet than the verses would bear.

CELIA. That's no matter; the feet might bear the verses.

ROSALIND. Ay, but the feet were lame, and could not bear themselves without the verse, and therefore stood lamely in the verse.

CELIA. But didst thou hear without wondering how thy name should be hanged and carved upon these trees?

ROSALIND. I was seven of the nine days out of the wonder before you came; for look here what I found on a palm-tree: I was never so be-rhymed since Pythagoras' time, that I was an Irish rat,[164] which I can hardly remember.

CELIA. Trow you who hath done this?

ROSALIND. Is it a man?

CELIA. And a chain, that you once wore, about his neck. Change you colour?

ROSALIND. I pray thee, who?

CELIA. O lord, lord! it is a hard matter for friends to meet; but mountains may be removed with earthquakes, and so encounter.[165]

ROSALIND. Nay, but who is it?

CELIA. Is it possible?

ROSALIND. Nay, I pr'ythee now, with most petitionary vehemence, tell me who it is.

CELIA. O wonderful, wonderful, most wonderful wonderful! and yet again wonderful, and after that, out of all whooping![166]

ROSALIND. Good my complection,[167] dost thou think, though I am caparisoned like a man, I have a doublet and hose in my disposition? One inch of delay more is a South-sea of discovery:[168] I pr'ythee tell me who is it? quickly, and speak apace. I would thou

---

[164] This romantic way of killing rats in Ireland is mentioned by Jonson and other writers of the time. So in the *Poetaster*: "Rhyme them to death, as they do Irish rats in drumming tunes."

[165] In Holland's Pliny, Shakespeare found that "two *hills* removed by an earthquake encountered together, charging as it were and with violence assaulting one another, and retiring again with a most mighty noise."

[166] To *whoop* or *hoop* is to cry out, to exclaim with astonishment. *Out of all cry* seems to have been a similar phrase for the expression of vehement admiration.

[167] "Good my complection" is merely a common inversion for "my good complection," like "good my lord," "dear my brother," "gentle my sister," &c. The phrase here means, no doubt, "my good wrapper-up of mystery"; as Celia has been tantalizing Rosalind "with half-told, half-withheld intelligence." *Complection* for *complicator*. For this explanation I am indebted to Mr. A. E. Brae.

[168] Here we have a tale of questions falling as thick as hail upon the devoted Celia. See how many things she is called upon to *discover*; and then say whether she has not incurred a laborious and vexatious duty by her *delay* in answering the first question. How plain it is that her *inch* of delay has cast her upon a *South Sea*—a vast and unexplored ocean—of discovery. The more Celia delays her revelation as to who the man is, the more she will have to reveal about him. Why? Because Rosalind fills up the delay (increases it, in fact) with fresh interrogatories, whereby Celia becomes lost in a South Sea of questions.—INGLEBY.

couldst stammer, that thou mightst pour this concealed man out of thy mouth, as wine comes out of narrow-mouth'd bottle,—either too much at once or none at all. I pr'ythee take the cork out of thy mouth that I may drink thy tidings.

CELIA. So you may put a man in your belly.

ROSALIND. Is he of God's making? What manner of man? Is his head worth a hat or his chin worth a beard?

CELIA. Nay, he hath but a little beard.

ROSALIND. Why, God will send more if the man will be thankful: let me stay the growth of his beard, if thou delay me not the knowledge of his chin.

CELIA. It is young Orlando, that tripped up the wrestler's heels and your heart both in an instant.

ROSALIND. Nay, but the devil take mocking: speak sad brow and true maid.[169]

CELIA. I' faith, coz, 'tis he.

ROSALIND. Orlando?

CELIA. Orlando.

ROSALIND. Alas the day! what shall I do with my doublet and hose? What did he when thou saw'st him? What said he? How look'd he? Wherein went he?[170] What makes he here?[171] Did he ask for me? Where remains he? How parted he with thee? and when shalt thou see him again? Answer me in one word.

CELIA. You must borrow me Gargantua's mouth first:[172] 'tis a word too great for any mouth of this age's size. To say ay and no to these particulars is more than to answer in a catechism.

ROSALIND. But doth he know that I am in this forest, and in man's apparel? Looks he as freshly as he did the day he wrestled?

CELIA. It is as easy to count atomies[173] as to resolve the propositions of a lover:—but take a taste of my finding him, and relish it with good observance. I found him under a tree, like a dropp'd acorn.

ROSALIND. It may well be called Jove's tree, when it drops forth such fruit.

CELIA. Give me audience, good madam.

ROSALIND. Proceed.

CELIA. There lay he, stretched along like a wounded knight.

ROSALIND. Though it be pity to see such a sight, it well becomes the

---

[169] Speak with a *serious* countenance, and as a true virgin.

[170] "How was he *dressed*?"

[171] "What *makes* he here?" is "What *is* he *doing* here?" or "What is his *business* here?" just as before, in the first scene, note 145.

[172] Gargantua is the name of a most gigantic giant in Rabelais, who forks five pilgrims, staves and all, into his mouth in a salad, and afterwards picks them out from between his teeth; not *swallows* them, as White says.

[173] "An *atomie* is a mote flying in the sun. Any thing so small that it cannot be made less." Bullokar's *English Expositor*, 1616.

ground.

CELIA. Cry, holla![174] to thy tongue, I pr'ythee; it curvets unseasonably. He was furnished like a hunter.

ROSALIND. O, ominous! he comes to kill my heart.[175]

CELIA. I would sing my song without a burden: thou bring'st me out of tune.

ROSALIND. Do you not know I am a woman? when I think, I must speak. Sweet, say on.

CELIA. You bring me out.—Soft! comes he not here?

ROSALIND. 'Tis he: slink by, and note him.

[CELIA *and* ROSALIND *retire.*]

[*Enter* ORLANDO *and* JAQUES.]

JAQUES. I thank you for your company; but, good faith, I had as lief have been myself alone.

ORLANDO. And so had I; but yet, for fashion's sake, I thank you too for your society.

JAQUES. God b' wi' you! let's meet as little as we can.

ORLANDO. I do desire we may be better strangers.

JAQUES. I pray you, mar no more trees with writing love songs in their barks.

ORLANDO. I pray you, mar no more of my verses with reading them ill-favouredly.

JAQUES. Rosalind is your love's name?

ORLANDO. Yes, just.

JAQUES. I do not like her name.

ORLANDO. There was no thought of pleasing you when she was christened.

JAQUES. What stature is she of?

ORLANDO. Just as high as my heart.

JAQUES. You are full of pretty answers. Have you not been acquainted with goldsmiths' wives, and conned them out of rings?[176]

ORLANDO. Not so; but I answer you right painted cloth,[177] from whence you have studied your questions.

JAQUES. You have a nimble wit: I think 'twas made of Atalanta's

---

[174] This was a term by which the rider restrained and *stopped* his horse.

[175] A quibble between *hart* and *heart*, then spelt the same.

[176] The meaning is, that goldsmiths' wives have given him the freedom of their husbands' shops, where he has committed to memory the mottoes inscribed on their rings and other jewels.

[177] To answer *right painted cloth* is to answer sententiously. *Painted cloth* was a species of hangings for the walls of rooms, which was cloth *painted* with various devices and mottoes. The verses, mottoes, and proverbial sentences on such cloths are often made the subject of allusion in old writers.

heels.[178] Will you sit down with me? and we two will rail against our mistress the world, and all our misery.

ORLANDO. I will chide no breather in the world but myself, against whom I know most faults.

JAQUES. The worst fault you have is to be in love.

ORLANDO. 'Tis a fault I will not change for your best virtue. I am weary of you.

JAQUES. By my troth, I was seeking for a Fool when I found you.

ORLANDO. He is drowned in the brook; look but in, and you shall see him.

JAQUES. There I shall see mine own figure.

ORLANDO. Which I take to be either a Fool or a cipher.

JAQUES. I'll tarry no longer with you: farewell, good Signior Love.

ORLANDO. I am glad of your departure: adieu, good Monsieur Melancholy. [*Exit* JAQUES. [CELIA *and* ROSALIND *come forward.*]

ROSALIND. [*Aside to* CELIA.] I will speak to him like a saucy lackey, and under that habit play the knave with him.—Do you hear, forester?

ORLANDO. Very well: what would you?

ROSALIND. I pray you, what is't o'clock?

ORLANDO. You should ask me what time o' day; there's no clock in the forest.

ROSALIND. Then there is no true lover in the forest, else sighing every minute and groaning every hour would detect the lazy foot of time as well as a clock.

ORLANDO. And why not the swift foot of time? had not that been as proper?

ROSALIND. By no means, sir. Time travels in divers paces with divers persons. I'll tell you who time ambles withal, who time trots withal, who time gallops withal, and who he stands still withal.

ORLANDO. I pr'ythee, who doth he trot withal?

ROSALIND. Marry, he trots hard with a young maid between the contract of her marriage and the day it is solemnized;[179] if the interim be but a se'nnight, time's pace is so hard that it seems the length of seven year.

ORLANDO. Who ambles time withal?

ROSALIND. With a priest that lacks Latin and a rich man that hath not the gout: for the one sleeps easily because he cannot study, and the

---

[178] The nimble-footedness of Atalanta has been referred to before, note 162.

[179] Hardly any thing is so apt to make a short journey *seem* long, as riding on a hard-trotting horse, however fast the horse may go. On the other hand, to ride an ambling horse makes a long journey seem short, because the horse rides so easy. It were hardly needful to say this, but that some have lately proposed to invert the order of the nags in this case.

other lives merrily because he feels no pain; the one lacking the
burden of lean and wasteful learning, the other knowing no burden
of heavy tedious penury. These time ambles withal.

ORLANDO. Who doth he gallop withal?

ROSALIND. With a thief to the gallows; for though he go as softly as
foot can fall, he thinks himself too soon there.

ORLANDO. Who stays it still withal?

ROSALIND. With lawyers in the vacation; for they sleep between term
and term, and then they perceive not how time moves.

ORLANDO. Where dwell you, pretty youth?

ROSALIND. With this shepherdess, my sister; here in the skirts of the
forest, like fringe upon a petticoat.

ORLANDO. Are you native of this place?

ROSALIND. As the cony, that you see dwell where she is kindled.[180]

ORLANDO. Your accent is something finer than you could purchase in
so removed[181] a dwelling.

ROSALIND. I have been told so of many: but indeed an old religious
uncle of mine taught me to speak, who was in his youth an inland
man; one that knew courtship[182] too well, for there he fell in love. I
have heard him read many lectures against it; and I thank God I am
not a woman, to be touched with so many giddy offences as he
hath generally taxed their whole sex withal.

ORLANDO. Can you remember any of the principal evils that he laid
to the charge of women?

ROSALIND. There were none principal; they were all like one another
as halfpence are; every one fault seeming monstrous till his fellow
fault came to match it.

ORLANDO. I pr'ythee recount some of them.

ROSALIND. No; I will not cast away my physic but on those that are
sick. There is a man haunts the forest that abuses our young plants
with carving *Rosalind* on their barks; hangs odes upon hawthorns,
and elegies on brambles; all, forsooth, deifying the name of
Rosalind: if I could meet that fancy-monger, I would give him
some good counsel, for he seems to have the quotidian[183] of love
upon him.

ORLANDO. I am he that is so love-shaked: I pray you tell me your
remedy.

---

[180] *Kindled*, here, is altogether another word than our present verb *to kindle*. It is
from *kind*, which, again, is from a word meaning *to bring forth*. The word has long been
obsolete.

[181] *Removed* is *sequestered*, *solitary*, or *lonely*; without neighbours.

[182] *Courtship* is the practice of Courts; *courtliness.*

[183] *Quotidian* was the name of an intermittent fever, so called because the fits came
on every day. In like manner, *tertian* and *quartan* were applied to those that came on
once in three and once in four days.

ROSALIND. There is none of my uncle's marks upon you; he taught me how to know a man in love; in which cage of rushes I am sure you are not prisoner.

ORLANDO. What were his marks?

ROSALIND. A lean cheek,—which you have not; a blue eye[184] and sunken,—which you have not: an unquestionable spirit,[185]—which you have not: a beard neglected; which you have not: but I pardon you for that, for simply your having in beard is a younger brother's revenue:[186]—then your hose should be ungartered, your bonnet unbanded, your sleeve unbuttoned, your shoe untied, and every thing about you demonstrating a careless desolation. But you are no such man; you are rather point-devise[187] in your accoutrements, as loving yourself than seeming the lover of any other.

ORLANDO. Fair youth, I would I could make thee believe I love.

ROSALIND. Me believe it! you may as soon make her that you love believe it; which, I warrant, she is apter to do than to confess she does: that is one of the points in the which women still give the lie to their consciences. But, in good sooth, are you he that hangs the verses on the trees, wherein Rosalind is so admired?

ORLANDO. I swear to thee, youth, by the white hand of Rosalind, I am that he, that unfortunate he.

ROSALIND. But are you so much in love as your rhymes speak?

ORLANDO. Neither rhyme nor reason can express how much.

ROSALIND. Love is merely a madness; and, I tell you, deserves as well a dark house and a whip as madmen do:[188] and the reason why they are not so punished and cured is, that the lunacy is so ordinary that the whippers are in love too. Yet I profess curing it by counsel.

ORLANDO. Did you ever cure any so?

ROSALIND. Yes, one; and in this manner. He was to imagine me his love, his mistress; and I set him every day to woo me: at which time would I, being but a moonish[189] youth, grieve, be effeminate, changeable, longing and liking; proud, fantastical, apish, shallow, inconstant, full of tears, full of smiles; for every passion something and for no passion truly anything, as boys and women are for the most part cattle of this colour; would now like him, now loathe

---

[184] Not blue in our sense of the phrase; but with blueness *about* the eyes, such as to indicate hunger or dejection. Blue eyes were called *gray* in the Poet's time.

[185] A reserved, unsociable spirit, the reverse of that in *Hamlet*: "Thou comest in such a *questionable* shape that I will speak to thee."

[186] Under the law of primogeniture, a younger brother's revenue was apt to be small. Orlando is too young for his *having* in beard to amount to much.

[187] That is, *precise, exact*; dressed with finical nicety.

[188] This shows how lunatics were apt to be treated in the Poet's time. But then lunacy was often counterfeited, as it still is, either as a cover to crime or as an occasion for charity.

[189] As changeable as the Moon.

him; then entertain him, then forswear him; now weep for him, then spit at him; that I drave my suitor from his mad humour of love to a living humour of madness; which was, to forswear the full stream of the world and to live in a nook merely[190] monastic. And thus I cured him; and this way will I take upon me to wash your liver[191] as clean as a sound sheep's heart, that there shall not be one spot of love in't.

ORLANDO. I would not be cured, youth.

ROSALIND. I would cure you, if you would but call me Rosalind, and come every day to my cote and woo me.

ORLANDO. Now, by the faith of my love, I will: tell me where it is.

ROSALIND. Go with me to it, and I'll show it you: and, by the way, you shall tell me where in the forest you live. Will you go?

ORLANDO. With all my heart, good youth.

ROSALIND. Nay, you must call me Rosalind.—Come, sister, will you go? [*Exeunt.*]

SCENE III.

Another Part of the Forest.

[*Enter* TOUCHSTONE *and* AUDREY; JAQUES *behind.*]

TOUCHSTONE. Come apace, good Audrey:[192] I will fetch up your goats, Audrey. And how, Audrey? am I the man yet? Doth my simple feature content you?[193]

---

[190] *Merely*, here, is *entirely* or *absolutely*. The Poet often has it thus. And so *mere*, in a former scene: "Second childishness and *mere* oblivion."

[191] The *liver* was supposed to be the seat of the passions and affections, especially of *love* and *courage*. Shakespeare very often speaks of it so.

[192] *Apace* is *quickly* or *fast.—Audrey* is a corruption of *Etheldreda*; the saint of that name being so styled in ancient calendars.

[193] In explanation of this passage, Mr. Joseph Crosby writes me as follows: "Mr. W. Wilkins, of Trinity College, Dublin, has recently pointed out that *feature* formerly meant a literary work, a poem, a drama, &c., just as we now call such a work *a composition*; being from the Latin verb *facere*, to *make*. Ben Jonson uses the word in this sense when he says of his creation, the play of *Volpone*, that two months before it was no *feature*:

To this there needs no lie, but this his creature,
Which was two months since no *feature*;
And, though he dares give them five lives to mend it,
'Tis known, five weeks fully penn'd it.

Various other examples of the use of this word in the sense of a literary production have been discovered, even as far back as the time of Pliny, who, in the Preface to his *Natural History*, speaks of his work as 'libri nati apud me proxima *fetura*.'" Then, referring to the passage in the text, Mr. Crosby continues: "From the context we find that Touchstone calls himself 'a poet,' and is nettled because his verses 'cannot be understood,' and

AUDREY. Your features! Lord warrant us! what features?

TOUCHSTONE. I am here with thee and thy goats, as the most capricious poet, honest Ovid, was among the Goths.[194]

JAQUES. [*Aside.*] O knowledge ill-inhabited,—worse than Jove in a thatch'd house![195]

TOUCHSTONE. When a man's verses cannot be understood, nor a man's good wit seconded with the forward child understanding, it strikes a man more dead than a great reckoning in a little room.[196]—Truly, I would the gods had made thee poetical.

AUDREY. I do not know what *poetical* is: is it honest in deed and word? is it a true thing?

TOUCHSTONE. No, truly: for the truest poetry is the most feigning; and lovers are given to poetry; and what they swear in poetry may be said, as lovers, they do feign.

AUDREY. Do you wish, then, that the gods had made me poetical?

TOUCHSTONE. I do, truly, for thou swear'st to me thou art honest; now, if thou wert a poet, I might have some hope thou didst feign.

AUDREY. Would you not have me honest?

TOUCHSTONE. No, truly, unless thou wert hard-favoured; for honesty coupled to beauty is to have honey a sauce to sugar.

JAQUES. [*Aside.*] A material Fool![197]

---

laments that the gods had not made his rustic adorer 'poetical.' Here, instead of asking, as the question is commonly supposed to signify, 'How does my intelligent countenance strike you now?' it is evident that, being a clown of brains and observation, he had been making love, as he had seen it done 'at Court,' by sending 'good Audrey' a poetical billet-doux; and his question means, 'How are you pleased with my love-ditty?' He tells us elsewhere that he 'could rhyme you eight years together, dinners and suppers and sleeping-hours excepted'; and no wonder he felt chagrined that his 'simple feature,' as he modestly terms his love-rhymes, was unregarded, and his 'good wit' thrown away, 'not being seconded with the forward child, understanding.' It was not his good looks that the clever and sharp-witted fellow was sensitive about: Audrey could have had no trouble to understand *them*: it was the non-appreciation of his gallant *poetical* 'feature' that disgusted him, and struck him 'more dead than a great reckoning in a little room.'

[194] Shakespeare remembered that *caper* was Latin for goat, and thence chose this epithet. There is also a quibble between *goats* and *Goths.*

[195] We have already had *disputable* for *disputatious*, and *unexpressive* for *inexpressible.* So here we have *ill-inhabited* for *ill-inhabiting*; that is, *ill-lodged.* An old classical fable represents that Jupiter and Mercury were once overtaken by night in Phrygia, and were inhospitably excluded by all the people, till at last an old poor couple, named Philemon and Baucis, who lived in a *thatched house*, took them in, and gave them the best entertainment the house would afford. See page 37, note 145.

[196] Rabelais has a saying, that "there is only one quarter of an hour in human life passed ill, and that is between the calling for a reckoning and the paying it." A heavy bill for narrow quarters is apt to dash the spirits of tavern mirth. There is, as Singer remarks, "much humour in comparing the blank countenance of a disappointed poet or wit, whose effusions have not been comprehended, to that of the reveller who has to pay largely for his carousing."

[197] A *material Fool* is a Fool with matter in him.—*Honest* and *honesty* are here used for *chaste* and *chastity.* So in i. 2, of this play: "Those that she makes fair, she scarce makes *honest*; and those that she makes *honest*, she makes very ill-favoured."

AUDREY. Well, I am not fair; and therefore I pray the gods make me honest!

TOUCHSTONE. Truly, and to cast away honesty upon a foul slut were to put good meat into an unclean dish.

AUDREY. I am not a slut, though I thank the gods I am foul.[198]

TOUCHSTONE. Well, praised be the gods for thy foulness! sluttishness may come hereafter. But be it as it may be, I will marry thee: and to that end I have been with Sir[199] Oliver Martext, the vicar of the next village; who hath promised to meet me in this place of the forest, and to couple us.

JAQUES. [*Aside.*] I would fain see this meeting.

AUDREY. Well, the gods give us joy!

TOUCHSTONE. Amen. A man may, if he were of a fearful heart, stagger in this attempt; for here we have no temple but the wood, no assembly but horn-beasts. But what though? Courage! As horns are odious, they are necessary. It is said,—*Many a man knows no end of his goods*; right! many a man has good horns and knows no end of them. Well, that is the dowry of his wife; 'tis none of his own getting. Horns? Ever to poor men alone? No, no; the noblest deer hath them as huge as the rascal.[200] Is the single man therefore blessed? No: as a walled town is more worthier than a village, so is the forehead of a married man more honourable than the bare brow of a bachelor: and by how much defence is better than no skill, by so much is horn more precious than to want.[201] Here comes Sir Oliver.—

[*Enter* SIR OLIVER MARTEXT.]

Sir Oliver Martext, you are well met. Will you dispatch us here under this tree, or shall we go with you to your chapel?

MARTEXT. Is there none here to give the woman?

TOUCHSTONE. I will not take her on gift of any man.

MARTEXT. Truly, she must be given, or the marriage is not lawful.

JAQUES. [*Coming forward.*] Proceed, proceed; I'll give her.

TOUCHSTONE. Good even, good Master What-ye-call't: how do you, sir? You are very well met: God 'ild[202] you for your last company:

---

[198] Audrey uses *foul* as opposed to *fair*; that is, for *plain, homely*. She has good authority for doing so. Thus in Thomas's *History of Italy*: "If the maiden be *fair*, she is soon had, and little money given with her; if she be *foul*, they advance her with a better portion."

[199] *Sir* was in common use as a clerical title in Shakespeare's time, and long before. He has several instances of it; as, *Sir* Hugh, the Welsh parson.

[200] *Rascal*, as an epithet of deer, means *lean* and *out of season*.

[201] A quibble between *horn* as meaning the ornament which bachelors never have, and the same word as meaning the "horn of plenty."

[202] That is, "God *yield* you"; an old phrase for "God *reward* you."

I am very glad to see you:—even a toy in hand here, sir:—nay; pray be cover'd.[203]

JAQUES. Will you be married, motley?

TOUCHSTONE. As the ox hath his bow,[204] sir, the horse his curb, and the falcon her bells, so man hath his desires; and as pigeons bill, so wedlock would be nibbling.

JAQUES. And will you, being a man of your breeding, be married under a bush, like a beggar? Get you to church and have a good priest that can tell you what marriage is: this fellow will but join you together as they join wainscot; then one of you will prove a shrunk panel, and like green timber, warp, warp.

TOUCHSTONE. [*Aside.*] I am not in the mind but I were better to be married of him than of another: for he is not like to marry me well; and not being well married, it will be a good excuse for me hereafter to leave my wife.

JAQUES. Go thou with me, and let me counsel thee.

TOUCHSTONE. Come, sweet Audrey;
We must be married or we must live in bawdry.—
Farewell, good Master Oliver:—not,

O sweet Oliver, O brave Oliver,
Leave me not behind thee;—

but,—

Wend away; be gone, I say,
I will not to wedding with thee.[205]

[*Exeunt* JAQUES, TOUCHSTONE, *and* AUDREY.]

MARTEXT. 'Tis no matter; ne'er a fantastical knave of them all shall flout me out of my calling. [*Exit.*]

---

[203] Jaques is supposed to be standing with his hat off, out of deference to the present company.

[204] His *yoke*, which, in ancient time, resembled a bow or branching horns.

[205] The ballad of "O sweet Oliver, leave me not behind thee," and the answer to it, are entered on the Stationers' books in 1584 and 1586. Touchstone says, I will sing, *not* that part of the ballad which says, "Leave me not behind thee"; *but* that which says, "Be gone, I say," probably pan of the answer.

SCENE IV.

Another Part of the Forest. Before a Cottage.

[*Enter* ROSALIND *and* CELIA.]

ROSALIND. Never talk to me; I will weep.

CELIA. Do, I pr'ythee; but yet have the grace to consider that tears do
not become a man.

ROSALIND. But have I not cause to weep?

CELIA. As good cause as one would desire; therefore weep.

ROSALIND. His very hair is of the dissembling colour.

CELIA. Something browner than Judas's:[206] marry, his kisses are
Judas's own children.

ROSALIND. I' faith, his hair is of a good colour.

CELIA. An excellent colour: your chestnut was ever the only colour.

ROSALIND. And his kissing is as full of sanctity as the touch of holy
bread.

CELIA. He hath bought a pair of cast lips of Diana: a nun of winter's
sisterhood kisses not more religiously; the very ice of chastity is in
them.

ROSALIND. But why did he swear he would come this morning, and
comes not?

CELIA. Nay, certainly, there is no truth in him.

ROSALIND. Do you think so?

CELIA. Yes; I think he is not a pick-purse nor a horse-stealer; but for
his verity in love, I do think him as concave as a covered goblet or
a worm-eaten nut.

ROSALIND. Not true in love?

CELIA. Yes, when he is in; but I think he is not in.

ROSALIND. You have heard him swear downright he was.

CELIA. *Was* is not *is*: besides, the oath of a lover is no stronger than
the word of a tapster;[207] they are both the confirmer of false
reckonings. He attends here in the forest on the Duke, your father.

ROSALIND. I met the Duke yesterday, and had much question[208] with
him. He asked me of what parentage I was; I told him, of as good
as he; so he laughed and let me go. But what talk we of fathers
when there is such a man as Orlando?

CELIA. O, that's a brave man! he writes brave verses, speaks brave
words, swears brave oaths, and breaks them bravely, quite traverse,

---

[206] Judas was represented in old paintings and tapestry, with red *hair* and *beard*. So
in *The Insatiate Countess*: "I ever thought by his *red beard* he would prove a *Judas.*"

[207] So the ancient proverb, "At lovers' perjuries Jove laughs."

[208] *Question*, here, is *talk* or *conversation.*

athwart the heart of his lover; as a puny tilter, that spurs his horse
but on one side, breaks his staff like a noble goose:[209] but all's
brave that youth mounts and folly guides.—Who comes here?

[*Enter* CORIN.]

CORIN. Mistress and master, you have oft enquired
After the shepherd that complain'd of love,
Who you saw sitting by me on the turf,
Praising the proud disdainful shepherdess
That was his mistress.
CELIA. Well, and what of him?
CORIN. If you will see a pageant truly play'd
Between the pale complexion of true love
And the red glow of scorn and proud disdain,
Go hence a little, and I shall conduct you,
If you will mark it.
ROSALIND. O, come, let us remove:
The sight of lovers feedeth those in love.—
Bring us to this sight, and you shall say
I'll prove a busy actor in their play. [*Exeunt.*]

SCENE V.

Another Part of the Forest.

[*Enter* SILVIUS *and* PHEBE.]

SILVIUS. Sweet Phebe, do not scorn me; do not, Phebe:
Say that you love me not; but say not so
In bitterness. The common executioner,
Whose heart the accustom'd sight of death makes hard,
Falls not the axe upon the humbled neck
But first begs pardon:[210] Will you sterner be
Than he that dies and lives by bloody drops?[211]

---

[209] An allusion to tilting, where it was held disgraceful for a knight to break his lance *across* the body of his adversary, instead of by a push of the point.

[210] It was customary for the executioner to kneel down and ask pardon of the victim, before striking him.—Here, again, *but begs* means *without begging.*

[211] This is a phrase of frequent occurrence in old writers, and seems to have been a common *hysteron-proteron* for *to live and die.* Its meaning has been somewhat disputed. One explanation is, "subsist from the cradle to the grave"; another, "being constant to a thing to the end." I prefer the explanation given by Dr. Sebastian Evans to Dr. C. M. Ingleby: "It means of course, to *make the thing a matter of life and death.* The profession or calling of a man is that of *which he dies and lives*; that is, by which he lives, and failing which he dies."

[*Enter* ROSALIND, CELIA, *and* CORIN, *behind.*]

PHEBE. I would not be thy executioner:
    I fly thee, for I would not injure thee.
    Thou tell'st me there is murder in mine eye:
    'Tis pretty, sure, and very probable,
    That eyes—that are the frail'st and softest things,
    Who shut their coward gates on atomies—
    Should be called tyrants, butchers, murderers!
    Now I do frown on thee with all my heart;
    And if mine eyes can wound, now let them kill thee:
    Now counterfeit to swoon; why, now fall down;
    Or, if thou canst not, O, for shame, for shame,
    Lie not, to say mine eyes are murderers.
    Now show the wound mine eye hath made in thee:
    Scratch thee but with a pin, and there remains
    Some scar of it; lean upon a rush,
    The cicatrice and capable impressure[212]
    Thy palm some moment keeps; but now mine eyes,
    Which I have darted at thee, hurt thee not;
    Nor, I am sure, there is not force in eyes
    That can do hurt.
SILVIUS. O dear Phebe,
    If ever—as that ever may be near—
    You meet in some fresh cheek the power of fancy,[213]
    Then shall you know the wounds invisible
    That love's keen arrows make.
PHEBE. But till that time
    Come not thou near me; and when that time comes
    Afflict me with thy mocks, pity me not;
    As till that time I shall not pity thee.
ROSALIND. [*Coming forward.*] And why, I pray you? Who might be
    your mother,
    That you insult, exult, and all at once,
    Over the wretched? What though you have no beauty,—
    As, by my faith, I see no more in you
    Than without candle may go dark to bed,—
    Must you be therefore proud and pitiless?[214]

---

[212] *Cicatrice* is *scar*, or *skin-mark. Capable impressure* is *sensible impression*. So the Poet has *incapable* for *insensible* or *unconscious*; *Hamlet*, 1v. 4: "As one incapable of her own distress."

[213] The use of *fancy* for *love* is very frequent in Shakespeare.

[214] Rosalind knows that to tell Phebe she ought not to be proud because she has beauty, would but make her the prouder; she therefore tells her she ought not to be proud

Why, what means this? Why do you look on me?
I see no more in you than in the ordinary
Of nature's sale-work:[215]—'Od's my little life,[216]
I think she means to tangle my eyes too!—
No, faith, proud mistress, hope not after it;
'Tis not your inky brows, your black silk hair,
Your bugle eyeballs, nor your cheek of cream,
That can entame my spirits to your worship.—
You foolish shepherd, wherefore do you follow her,
Like foggy south, puffing with wind and rain?
You are a thousand times a properer[217] man
Than she a woman. 'Tis such fools as you
That makes the world full of ill-favour'd children:
'Tis not her glass, but you, that flatters her;
And out of you she sees herself more proper
Than any of her lineaments can show her.—
But, mistress, know yourself; down on your knees,
And thank Heaven, fasting, for a good man's love:
For I must tell you friendly in your ear,—
Sell when you can; you are not for all markets:
Cry the man mercy;[218] love him; take his offer;
Foul is most foul, being foul to be a scoffer.[219]—
So take her to thee, shepherd:—fare you well.
PHEBE. Sweet youth, I pray you chide a year together:
I had rather hear you chide than this man woo.
ROSALIND. He's fallen in love with your foulness, and she'll fall in
love with my anger:—if it be so, as fast as she answers thee with
frowning looks, I'll sauce her with bitter words.—Why look you so
upon me?
PHEBE. For no ill-will I bear you.
ROSALIND. I pray you do not fall in love with me,
For I am falser than vows made in wine:
Besides, I like you not.—If you will know my house,
'Tis at the tuft of olives here hard by.—
Will you go, sister?—Shepherd, ply her hard.—
Come, sister.—Shepherdess, look on him better,

---

because she lacks it. The best way to take down people's pride often is, to assume that
they cannot be so big fools as to think they have any thing to be proud of.

[215] Meaning, apparently, work made for the general market, and not to particular
order or for any special purpose or purchaser.

[216] A petty oath; *'Od's* being a diminutive or disguise of *God's*.

[217] *Proper*, again, for handsome. See page 10, note 41.

[218] To *cry* one *mercy* is to *ask* his *pardon*. A frequent usage.

[219] *To be* is another instance of the infinitive used gerundively. So that the meaning
is, the ugly are most ugly when they add further ugliness *by being* scoffers. See page 11,
note 48.

And be not proud; though all the world could see,
None could be so abused in sight as he.[220]—
Come to our flock. [*Exeunt* ROSALIND, CELIA, *and* CORIN.]
PHEBE. Dead shepherd! now I find thy saw of might;
    Who ever loved that loved not at first sight?[221]
SILVIUS. Sweet Phebe,—
PHEBE. Ha! what say'st thou, Silvius?
SILVIUS. Sweet Phebe, pity me.
PHEBE. Why, I am sorry for thee, gentle Silvius.
SILVIUS. Wherever sorrow is, relief would be:
    If you do sorrow at my grief in love,
    By giving love, your sorrow and my grief
    Were both extermin'd.
PHEBE. Thou hast my love: is not that neighbourly?
SILVIUS. I would have you.
PHEBE. Why, that were covetousness.
    Silvius, the time was that I hated thee;
    And yet it is not that I bear thee love:
    But since that thou canst talk of love so well,
    Thy company, which erst was irksome to me,
    I will endure; and I'll employ thee too:
    But do not look for further recompense
    Than thine own gladness that thou art employ'd.
SILVIUS. So holy and so perfect is my love,
    And I in such a poverty of grace,
    That I shall think it a most plenteous crop
    To glean the broken ears after the man
    That the main harvest reaps: lose now and then
    A scatter'd smile, and that I'll live upon.
PHEBE. Know'st thou the youth that spoke to me erewhile?
SILVIUS. Not very well; but I have met him oft;
    And he hath bought the cottage and the bounds
    That the old carlot[222] once was master of.
PHEBE. Think not I love him, though I ask for him;
    'Tis but a peevish boy:—yet he talks well;—
    But what care I for words? yet words do well
    When he that speaks them pleases those that hear.

---

[220] "If all men could see you, none but he could be so *deceived* as to think you beautiful." To *abuse* often has that sense.

[221] This line is from Marlowe's translation of *Hero and Leander*, which was not printed till 1598, though the author was killed in 1593. The poem was deservedly popular, and the words "dead shepherd" look as though Shakespeare remembered him with affection.

[222] *Churl, carle,* and *carlot* are all words of the same origin and meaning. The same person has already been described as "of a *churlish* disposition."

It is a pretty youth:—not very pretty:—
But, sure, he's proud; and yet his pride becomes him:
He'll make a proper man: the best thing in him
Is his complexion; and faster than his tongue
Did make offence, his eye did heal it up.
He is not very tall; yet for his years he's tall;
His leg is but so-so; and yet 'tis well:
There was a pretty redness in his lip;
A little riper and more lusty red
Than that mix'd in his cheek; 'twas just the difference
Betwixt the constant red and mingled damask.[223]
There be some women, Silvius, had they mark'd him
In parcels[224] as I did, would have gone near
To fall in love with him: but, for my part,
I love him not, nor hate him not; and yet
I have more cause to hate him than to love him:
For what had he to do to chide at me?[225]
He said mine eyes were black, and my hair black;
And, now I am remember'd, scorn'd at me:
I marvel why I answer'd not again:
But that's all one; omittance is no quittance.[226]
I'll write to him a very taunting letter,
And thou shalt bear it: wilt thou, Silvius?
SILVIUS. Phebe, with all my heart.
PHEBE. I'll write it straight,
The matter's in my head and in my heart:
I will be bitter with him and passing short:
Go with me, Silvius. [*Exeunt.*]

---

[223] Shakespeare has reference to the *red rose*, which is red all over alike, and the *damask rose*, in which various shades of colour are *mingled*.

[224] In *parcels* is *in detail*; part by part.

[225] That is, "What business had he to chide me?"

[226] *Quittance* is *acquittance, release,* or *discharge.* The saying appears to have been proverbial.

ACT IV.

SCENE I.

The Forest of Arden.

[*Enter* ROSALIND, CELIA, *and* JAQUES.]

JAQUES. I pr'ythee, pretty youth, let me be better acquainted with thee.

ROSALIND. They say you are a melancholy fellow.

JAQUES. I am so; I do love it better than laughing.

ROSALIND. Those that are in extremity of either are abominable fellows, and betray themselves to every modern[227] censure worse than drunkards.

JAQUES. Why, 'tis good to be sad and say nothing.

ROSALIND. Why then, 'tis good to be a post.

JAQUES. I have neither the scholar's melancholy, which is emulation; nor the musician's, which is fantastical; nor the courtier's, which is proud; nor the soldier's, which is ambitious; nor the lawyer's, which is politic; nor the lady's, which is nice;[228] nor the lover's, which is all these: but it is a melancholy of mine own, compounded of many simples,[229] extracted from many objects: and, indeed, the sundry contemplation of my travels; in which my often rumination wraps me in a most humorous sadness.

ROSALIND. A traveller! By my faith, you have great reason to be sad: I fear you have sold your own lands to see other men's; then to have seen much and to have nothing is to have rich eyes and poor hands.

JAQUES. Yes, I have gained my experience.

ROSALIND. And your experience makes you sad: I had rather have a Fool to make me merry than experience to make me sad; and to travel for it too.

[*Enter* ORLANDO.]

ORLANDO. Good day and happiness, dear Rosalind!

JAQUES. Nay, then, God b' wi' you, an you talk in blank verse.

ROSALIND. Farewell, Monsieur Traveller: look you lisp and wear

---

[227] *Modern*, again, for *common* or *ordinary.* See page 34, note 135.—*Extremity*, in the line before, is *excess* or *too much.*

[228] *Nice* here means *fastidious, dainty,* or *squeamish.* Repeatedly so.

[229] *Simples* is the old word for *herbs*; here it has the sense of *elements.*

strange suits; disable[230] all the benefits of your own country; be out of love with your nativity, and almost chide God for making you that countenance you are; or I will scarce think you have swam in a gondola.[231] [*Exit* JAQUES.]—Why, how now, Orlando! where have you been all this while? You a lover!—An you serve me such another trick, never come in my sight more.

ORLANDO. My fair Rosalind, I come within an hour of my promise.

ROSALIND. Break an hour's promise in love! He that will divide a minute into a thousand parts, and break but a part of the thousand part of a minute in the affairs of love, it may be said of him that Cupid hath clapped him o' the shoulder, but I'll warrant him heart-whole.

ORLANDO. Pardon me, dear Rosalind.

ROSALIND. Nay, an you be so tardy, come no more in my sight: I had as lief be wooed of a snail.

ORLANDO. Of a snail!

ROSALIND. Ay, of a snail; for though he comes slowly, he carries his house on his head,—a better jointure, I think, than you make a woman: besides, he brings his destiny with him.

ORLANDO. What's that?

ROSALIND. Why, horns; which such as you are fain to be beholding to your wives for: but he comes armed in his fortune, and prevents[232] the slander of his wife.

ORLANDO. Virtue is no horn-maker; and my Rosalind is virtuous.

ROSALIND. And I am your Rosalind.

CELIA. It pleases him to call you so; but he hath a Rosalind of a better leer[233] than you.

ROSALIND. Come, woo me, woo me; for now I am in a holiday humour, and like enough to consent.—What would you say to me now, an I were your very, very Rosalind?

ORLANDO. I would kiss before I spoke.

ROSALIND. Nay, you were better speak first; and when you were gravell'd[234] for lack of matter, you might take occasion to kiss. Very good orators, when they are out, they will spit; and for lovers lacking (God warn us!) matter, the cleanliest shift is to kiss.

ORLANDO. How if the kiss be denied?

ROSALIND. Then she puts you to entreaty, and there begins new

---

[230] *Disable* in the sense of *disparage, detract from,* or *depreciate.*

[231] In Shakespeare's time, Venice was the common resort of travellers, as much as Paris is now. And of course all who went to Venice sailed or "swam in a gondola."

[232] *Prevents* in its old sense of *anticipates.* The word literally means *goes before.*— "The slander of his wife" is the slander *caused by* his wife.

[233] Leer is *complexion, colour,* or *look*; much used in old metrical romances.

[234] This use of to *gravel* probably sprang from horses being lamed, as they sometimes are, by getting gravel-stones into their hoofs.

matter.

ORLANDO. Who could be out, being before his beloved mistress?

ROSALIND. Marry, that should you, if I were your mistress; or I should think my honesty ranker than my wit.

ORLANDO. What, of my suit?

ROSALIND. Not out of your apparel, and yet out of your suit. Am not I your Rosalind?

ORLANDO. I take some joy to say you are, because I would be talking of her.

ROSALIND. Well, in her person, I say I will not have you.

ORLANDO. Then, in mine own person, I die.

ROSALIND. No, faith, die by attorney.[235] The poor world is almost six thousand years old, and in all this time there was not any man died in his own person, *videlicet*, in a love-cause. Troilus had his brains dashed out with a Grecian club; yet he did what he could to die before; and he is one of the patterns of love. Leander, he would have lived many a fair year, though Hero had turned nun, if it had not been for a hot midsummer night; for, good youth, he went but forth to wash him in the Hellespont, and, being taken with the cramp, was drowned; and the foolish chroniclers of that age found it was—Hero of Sestos.[236] But these are all lies; men have died from time to time, and worms have eaten them, but not for love.

ORLANDO. I would not have my right Rosalind of this mind; for, I protest,[237] her frown might kill me.

ROSALIND. By this hand, it will not kill a fly. But come, now I will be your Rosalind in a more coming-on disposition;[238] and ask me what you will, I will grant it.

ORLANDO. Then love me, Rosalind.

ROSALIND. Yes, faith, will I, Fridays and Saturdays, and all.

ORLANDO. And wilt thou have me?

ROSALIND. Ay, and twenty such.

ORLANDO. What sayest thou?

ROSALIND. Are you not good?

ORLANDO. I hope so.

ROSALIND. Why then, can one desire too much of a good thing?—[*to Celia.*] Come, sister, you shall be the priest, and marry us.—Give me your hand, Orlando:—What do you say, sister?

ORLANDO. Pray thee, marry us.

---

[235] That is, by *deputy* or *substitute*. A man's *attorney* is one who represents him or stands for him in his cause.

[236] Found, brought in, a verdict of drowned himself for love of Hero. The report of the old chroniclers or historians is *implicitly* compared to the finding of a coroner's inquest.

[237] *Protest*, both verb and noun, is used for a strong affirmation.

[238] A disposition more facile, ready, and encouraging.

CELIA. I cannot say the words.

ROSALIND. You must begin, *Will you, Orlando,*—

CELIA. Go to.—Will you, Orlando, have to wife this Rosalind?

ORLANDO. I will.

ROSALIND. Ay, but when?

ORLANDO. Why, now; as fast as she can marry us.

ROSALIND. Then you must say,—*I take thee, Rosalind, for wife.*

ORLANDO. I take thee, Rosalind, for wife.

ROSALIND. I might ask you for your commission;[239] but,—I do take thee, Orlando, for my husband:—there's a girl goes before the priest;[240] and, certainly, a woman's thought runs before her actions.

ORLANDO. So do all thoughts; they are winged.

ROSALIND. Now tell me how long you would have her, after you have possessed her.

ORLANDO. For ever and a day.

ROSALIND. Say a day, without the ever. No, no, Orlando: men are April when they woo, December when they wed: maids are May when they are maids, but the sky changes when they are wives. I will be more jealous of thee than a Barbary cock-pigeon over his hen; more clamorous than a parrot against rain; more new-fangled than an ape; more giddy in my desires than a monkey: I will weep for nothing, like Diana in the fountain;[241] and I will do that when you are disposed to be merry; I will laugh like a hyen,[242] and that when thou are inclined to sleep.

ORLANDO. But will my Rosalind do so?

ROSALIND. By my life, she will do as I do.

ORLANDO. O, but she is wise.

ROSALIND. Or else she could not have the wit to do this: the wiser, the waywarder: make the doors[243] upon a woman's wit, and it will out at the casement; shut that, and it will out at the keyhole; stop that, 'twill fly with the smoke out at the chimney.

ORLANDO. A man that had a wife with such a wit, he might say,— *Wit, whither wilt?*[244]

ROSALIND. Nay, you might keep that check for it, till you met your

---

[239] That is, your *authority* to perform the marriage ceremony.

[240] Goes faster than the priest, gets ahead of him in the service; alluding to her anticipating what should be said first by Celia.

[241] Figures, and particularly that of *Diana,* with water conveyed through them, were anciently a frequent ornament of fountains. So in *The City Match*: "Now could I cry like any image in a fountain, which runs lamentations." Such an image of Diana, "with water *prilling* from her naked breast," was set up at the cross in Cheapside in 1596, according to Stowe.

[242] The bark of the hyæna was thought to resemble a loud laugh.

[243] Bar the doors, make them *fast.*

[244] "Wit, whither wilt?" is an old proverbial saying often met with in the early English writers.

wife's wit going to your neighbour's bed.

ORLANDO. And what wit could wit have to excuse that?

ROSALIND. Marry, to say, she came to seek you there. You shall never take her without her answer, unless you take her without her tongue. O, that woman that cannot make her fault her husband's occasion,[245] let her never nurse her child herself, for she will breed it like a Fool.

ORLANDO. For these two hours, Rosalind, I will leave thee.

ROSALIND. Alas, dear love, I cannot lack thee two hours!

ORLANDO. I must attend the Duke at dinner; by two o'clock I will be with thee again.

ROSALIND. Ay, go your ways, go your ways; I knew what you would prove; my friends told me as much, and I thought no less. That flattering tongue of yours won me: 'tis but one cast away, and so,—come death! Two o'clock is your hour?

ORLANDO. Ay, sweet Rosalind.

ROSALIND. By my troth, and in good earnest, and so God mend me, and by all pretty oaths that are not dangerous, if you break one jot of your promise, or come one minute behind your hour, I will think you the most pathetical[246] break-promise, and the most hollow lover, and the most unworthy of her you call Rosalind, that may be chosen out of the gross band of the unfaithful: therefore beware my censure, and keep your promise.

ORLANDO. With no less religion than if thou wert indeed my Rosalind: so, adieu!

ROSALIND. Well, Time is the old justice that examines all such offenders, and let time try: adieu! [*Exit* ORLANDO.]

CELIA. You have simply misused our sex in your love-prate: we must have your doublet and hose plucked over your head, and show the world what the bird hath done to her own nest.[247]

ROSALIND. O coz, coz, coz, my pretty little coz, that thou didst know how many fathom deep I am in love! But it cannot be sounded: my affection hath an unknown bottom, like the bay of Portugal.

CELIA. Or rather, bottomless; that as fast as you pour affection in, it runs out.

ROSALIND. No; that same wicked bastard of Venus, that was begot of thought, conceived of spleen, and born of madness; that blind rascally boy, that abuses every one's eyes, because his own are out, let him be judge how deep I am in love.—I'll tell thee, Aliena, I

---

[245] This, if it be the right text, must mean "represent or make out that her husband was the occasion of her fault."

[246] *Pathetical* sometimes had the sense of *impassioned.* Rosalind seems to be using it playfully, or with mock-seriousness.

[247] Referring to the old proverb, "'Tis an ill bird that fouls her own nest."

cannot be out of the sight of Orlando: I'll go find a shadow,[248] and sigh till he come.

CELIA. And I'll sleep. [*Exeunt.*]

SCENE II.

Another Part of the Forest.

[*Enter* JAQUES *and* Lords *in the habit of Foresters, with a dead deer.*]

JAQUES. Which is he that killed the deer?

1st LORD. Sir, it was I.

JAQUES. Let's present him to the Duke, like a Roman conqueror; and it would do well to set the deer's horns upon his head for a branch of victory.—Have you no song, forester, for this purpose?

2nd LORD. Yes, sir.

JAQUES. Sing it; 'tis no matter how it be in tune, so it make noise enough.

SONG.

2nd LORD.   *What shall he have that kill'd the deer?*
                His leather skin and horns to wear.

[*They sing him home, the rest bearing this burden.*]

                Then sing him home; the rest shall bear this burden.
                Take thou no scorn to wear the horn;
                It was a crest ere thou wast born.
                    Thy father's father wore it;
                    And thy father bore it;
                The horn, the horn, the lusty horn,
                Is not a thing to laugh to scorn. [*Exeunt.*]

---

[248] *Shadow* for *shade* or *shady place.* So in *The Tempest,* iv. 1: "And thy brown groves, whose *shadow* the dismissed bachelor loves."

SCENE III.

Another part of the Forest.

[*Enter* ROSALIND *and* CELIA.]

ROSALIND. How say you now? Is it not past two o'clock? And here
much[249] Orlando!
CELIA. I warrant you, with pure love and troubled brain, he hath ta'en
his bow and arrows, and is gone forth—to sleep. Look, who comes
here.

[*Enter* SILVIUS.]

SILVIUS. My errand is to you, fair youth:
My gentle Phebe did bid me give you this: [*Giving a letter.*]
I know not the contents; but, as I guess
By the stern brow and waspish action
Which she did use as she was writing of it,
It bears an angry tenor: pardon me,
I am but as a guiltless messenger.
ROSALIND. Patience herself would startle at this letter,
And play the swaggerer; bear this, bear all:
She says I am not fair; that I lack manners;
She calls me proud, and that she could not love me,
Were man as rare as Phoenix. Od's my will!
Her love is not the hare that I do hunt;
Why writes she so to me?—Well, shepherd, well,
This is a letter of your own device.
SILVIUS. No, I protest, I know not the contents:
Phebe did write it.
ROSALIND. Come, come, you are a Fool,
And turn'd into the extremity of love.
I saw her hand: she has a leathern hand,
A freestone-colour'd hand: I verily did think
That her old gloves were on, but 'twas her hands;
She has a housewife's hand: but that's no matter:
I say she never did invent this letter:
This is a man's invention, and his hand.
SILVIUS. Sure, it is hers.
ROSALIND. Why, 'tis a boisterous and a cruel style;

---

[249] *Much* is used ironically here; as we still say, "A good deal you will," meaning
"No you won't."

A style for challengers: why, she defies me,
Like Turk to Christian: women's gentle brain
Could not drop forth such giant-rude invention,
Such Ethiop words, blacker in their effect
Than in their countenance.—Will you hear the letter?
SILVIUS. So please you, for I never heard it yet;
Yet heard too much of Phebe's cruelty.
ROSALIND. She Phebes me: mark how the tyrant writes.

[*Reads.*]   *Art thou god to shepherd turn'd,*
               That a maiden's heart hath burn'd?—

Can a woman rail thus?
SILVIUS. Call you this railing?
ROSALIND. [*Reads.*]

               Why, thy godhead laid apart,
               Warr'st thou with a woman's heart?—

Did you ever hear such railing?

[*Reads.*]   *Whiles the eye of man did woo me,*
               That could do no vengeance to me.—

Meaning me a beast.—

[*Reads.*]   *If the scorn of your bright eyne*
               Have power to raise such love in mine,
               Alack, in me what strange effect
               Would they work in mild aspect?
               Whiles you chid me, I did love;
               How then might your prayers move?
               He that brings this love to thee
               Little knows this love in me:
               And by him seal up thy mind;[250]
               Whether that thy youth and kind[251]
               Will the faithful offer take
               Of me and all that I can make;
               Or else by him my love deny,
               And then I'll study how to die.

SILVIUS. Call you this chiding?

---

[250] "Seal up your answer, and send it back by him."
[251] *Kind*, again, in its radical sense of *nature*. See page 23, note 88.

CELIA. Alas, poor shepherd!

ROSALIND. Do you pity him? no, he deserves no pity.—Wilt thou love such a woman? What, to make thee an instrument, and play false strains upon thee! Not to be endured! Well, go your way to her,—for I see love hath made thee a tame snake,—and say this to her;—that if she love me, I charge her to love thee; if she will not, I will never have her unless thou entreat for her.—If you be a true lover, hence, and not a word; for here comes more company. [*Exit* SILVIUS.]

[*Enter* OLIVER.]

OLIVER. Good morrow, fair ones: pray you, if you know,
Where in the purlieus of this forest stands
A sheep-cote fenc'd about with olive trees?

CELIA. West of this place, down in the neighbour bottom:
The rank of osiers, by the murmuring stream,
Left on your right hand, brings you to the place.
But at this hour the house doth keep itself;
There's none within.

OLIVER. If that an eye may profit by a tongue,
Then should I know you by description;
Such garments, and such years: *The boy is fair,*
Of female favour, and bestows himself[252]
Like a ripe sister: the woman low,
And browner than her brother. Are not you
The owner of the house I did inquire for?

CELIA. It is no boast, being ask'd, to say we are.

OLIVER. Orlando doth commend him to you both;
And to that youth he calls his Rosalind
He sends this bloody napkin;[253]—are you he?

ROSALIND. I am: what must we understand by this?

OLIVER. Some of my shame; if you will know of me
What man I am, and how, and why, and where,
This handkerchief was stain'd.

CELIA. I pray you, tell it.

OLIVER. When last the young Orlando parted from you,
He left a promise to return again
Within an hour; and, pacing through the forest,
Chewing the food of sweet and bitter fancy,[254]

---

[252] "*Bestows* himself" is *bears* himself, *behaves*, or *appears.*

[253] *Napkin* and *handkerchief* were often used interchangeably.

[254] To *chew the cud* was a common phrase, meaning to *ruminate*, or *revolve in the mind.*—The epithets *sweet* and *bitter* are in accordance with the old custom of describing love by contraries; and we have many instances of *fancy* used for *love.*

Lo, what befell! he threw his eye aside,
And, mark, what object did present itself!
Under an oak, whose boughs were moss'd with age,
And high top bald with dry antiquity,
A wretched ragged man, o'ergrown with hair,
Lay sleeping on his back: about his neck
A green and gilded snake had wreath'd itself,
Who, with her head nimble in threats, approach'd
The opening of his mouth; but suddenly,
Seeing Orlando, it unlink'd itself,
And with indented glides did slip away
Into a bush: under which bush's shade
A lioness, with udders all drawn dry,
Lay couching, head on ground, with cat-like watch,
When that the sleeping man should stir; for 'tis
The royal disposition of that beast
To prey on nothing that doth seem as dead.[255]
This seen, Orlando did approach the man,
And found it was his brother, his elder brother.

CELIA. O, I have heard him speak of that same brother;
And he did render[256] him the most unnatural
That liv'd amongst men.

OLIVER. And well he might so do,
For well I know he was unnatural.

ROSALIND. But, to Orlando:—did he leave him there,
Food to the suck'd and hungry lioness?

OLIVER. Twice did he turn his back, and purpos'd so;
But kindness, nobler ever than revenge,
And nature, stronger than his just occasion,
Made him give battle to the lioness,
Who quickly fell before him; in which hurtling[257]
From miserable slumber I awaked.

CELIA. Are you his brother?

ROSALIND. Was it you he rescued?

CELIA. Was't you that did so oft contrive to kill him?

OLIVER. 'Twas I; but 'tis not I: I do not shame
To tell you what I was, since my conversion

---

[255] The bringing lions, serpents, palm-trees, rustic shepherds, and banished noblemen together in the Forest of Arden, is a strange piece of geographical license, which the critics have not failed to notice. I suspect the Poet knew well enough what he was about. The matter, however, was taken from Lodge's tale.

[256] *Render* here means *report* or *represent*. The Poet has it repeatedly in his sense, or in senses near akin to this.

[257] That is, jostling or clashing encounter. In *Julius Caesar* we have "The noise of battle *hurtled* in the air."

So sweetly tastes, being the thing I am.
ROSALIND. But, for the bloody napkin?—
OLIVER. By and by.
    When from the first to last, betwixt us two,
    Tears our recountments had most kindly bath'd,
    As, how I came into that desert place;—
    In brief, he led me to the gentle Duke,
    Who gave me fresh array and entertainment,
    Committing me unto my brother's love,
    Who led me instantly unto his cave,
    There stripp'd himself, and here upon his arm
    The lioness had torn some flesh away,
    Which all this while had bled; and now he fainted,
    And cried, in fainting, upon Rosalind.
    Brief, I recover'd him, bound up his wound,
    And, after some small space, being strong at heart,
    He sent me hither, stranger as I am,
    To tell this story, that you might excuse
    His broken promise, and to give this napkin,
    Dy'd in his blood, unto the shepherd-youth
    That he in sport doth call his Rosalind.

    [ROSALIND *faints.*]

CELIA. Why, how now, Ganymede! sweet Ganymede!
OLIVER. Many will swoon when they do look on blood.
CELIA. There is more in it:—Cousin!—Ganymede![258]
OLIVER. Look, he recovers.
ROSALIND. I would I were at home.
CELIA. We'll lead you thither.—
    I pray you, will you take him by the arm?
OLIVER. Be of good cheer, youth:—you a man?—You lack a man's
    heart.
ROSALIND. I do so, I confess it. Ah, sir, a body would think this was
    well counterfeited.[259] I pray you tell your brother how well I
    counterfeited.—Heigh-ho!—
OLIVER. This was not counterfeit; there is too great testimony in your
    complexion that it was a passion of earnest.
ROSALIND. Counterfeit, I assure you.

---

[258] In her sudden fright, Celia is betrayed out of her assumed character, and calls out "Cousin," then instantaneously corrects herself, lest she should start some suspicion as to what she or Rosalind is.

[259] Rosalind is afraid of being discovered; that her fainting will betray her; and in her anxiety to keep up the show of a saucy, mannish youth, perhaps she slightly overacts the part in this instance.

OLIVER. Well then, take a good heart, and counterfeit to be a man.
ROSALIND. So I do: but, i' faith, I should have been a woman by right.
CELIA. Come, you look paler and paler: pray you draw homewards.—
Good sir, go with us.
OLIVER. That will I, for I must bear answer back
How you excuse my brother, Rosalind.
ROSALIND. I shall devise something: but, I pray you, commend my
counterfeiting to him.—Will you go? [*Exeunt.*]

ACT V.

SCENE I.

The Forest of Arden.

[*Enter* TOUCHSTONE *and* AUDREY.]

TOUCHSTONE. We shall find a time, Audrey; patience, gentle
Audrey.
AUDREY. Faith, the priest was good enough, for all the old
gentleman's saying.
TOUCHSTONE. A most wicked Sir Oliver, Audrey, a most vile
Martext. But, Audrey, there is a youth here in the forest lays claim
to you.
AUDREY. Ay, I know who 'tis: he hath no interest in me in the world:
here comes the man you mean.
TOUCHSTONE. It is meat and drink to me to see a clown: By my
troth, we that have good wits have much to answer for; we shall be
flouting; we cannot hold.[260]

[*Enter* WILLIAM.]

WILLIAM. Good even, Audrey.
AUDREY. God ye good even,[261] William.
WILLIAM. And good even to you, sir.
TOUCHSTONE. Good even, gentle friend. Cover thy head, cover thy
head; nay, pr'ythee, be cover'd.[262] How old are you, friend?
WILLIAM. Five and twenty, sir.
TOUCHSTONE. A ripe age. Is thy name William?
WILLIAM. William, sir.
TOUCHSTONE. A fair name. Wast born i' the forest here?

---

[260] "Cannot *restrain* or *hold in* our wits."
[261] "God *give* you good even;" the original Salutation in the process of abbreviation
into "good even," or "good evening."
[262] William is standing with his hat off, in token of respect.

WILLIAM. Ay, sir, I thank God.
TOUCHSTONE. Thank God;—a good answer. Art rich?
WILLIAM. Faith, sir, so-so.
TOUCHSTONE. "So-so" is good, very good, very excellent good:—
and yet it is not; it is but so-so. Art thou wise?
WILLIAM. Ay, sir, I have a pretty wit.
TOUCHSTONE. Why, thou say'st well. I do now remember a saying;
*The fool doth think he is wise, but the wise man knows himself to
be a fool.* The heathen philosopher, when he had a desire to eat a
grape, would open his lips when he put it into his mouth; meaning
thereby that grapes were made to eat and lips to open. You do love
this maid?
WILLIAM. I do, sir.
TOUCHSTONE. Give me your hand. Art thou learnèd?
WILLIAM. No, sir.
TOUCHSTONE. Then learn this of me: To have is to have; for it is a
figure in rhetoric that drink, being poured out of cup into a glass,
by filling the one doth empty the other; for all your writers do
consent that ipse is he; now, you are not *ipse*, for I am he.
WILLIAM. Which he, sir?
TOUCHSTONE. He, sir, that must marry this woman. Therefore, you
clown, abandon,—which is in the vulgar, leave,—the society,—
which in the boorish is company,—of this female,—which in the
common is woman,—which together is abandon the society of this
female; or, clown, thou perishest; or, to thy better understanding,
diest; or, to wit, I kill thee, make thee away, translate thy life into
death, thy liberty into bondage: I will deal in poison with thee, or
in bastinado, or in steel; I will bandy with thee in faction;[263] will
o'er-run thee with policy;[264] I will kill thee a hundred and fifty
ways; therefore tremble and depart.
AUDREY. Do, good William.
WILLIAM. God rest you merry,[265] sir. [*Exit.*]

[*Enter* CORIN.]

CORIN. Our master and mistress seek you; come away, away!
TOUCHSTONE. Trip, Audrey, trip, Audrey;—I attend, I attend.
[*Exeunt.*]

---

[263] "Fight against thee with conspiracies."
[264] "Circumvent thee with cunning;" the art of politicians.
[265] "God *keep* you merry," or "*let* you *continue* merry."

SCENE II.

Another Part of the Forest.

[*Enter* ORLANDO *and* OLIVER.]

ORLANDO. Is't possible that on so little acquaintance you should like
her? that but seeing you should love her? and loving woo? and,
wooing, she should grant? and will you persever to enjoy her?

OLIVER. Neither call the giddiness of it in question, the poverty of her,
the small acquaintance, my sudden wooing, nor her sudden
consenting; but say with me, I love Aliena; say, with her, that she
loves me; consent with both, that we may enjoy each other: it shall
be to your good; for my father's house, and all the revenue that
was old Sir Rowland's will I estate upon you, and here live and die
a shepherd.

ORLANDO. You have my consent. Let your wedding be to-morrow:
thither will I invite the Duke and all's contented followers. Go you
and prepare Aliena; for, look you, here comes my Rosalind.

[*Enter* ROSALIND.]

ROSALIND. God save you, brother.

OLIVER. And you, fair sister.[266] [*Exit.*]

ROSALIND. O, my dear Orlando, how it grieves me to see thee wear
thy heart in a scarf!

ORLANDO. It is my arm.

ROSALIND. I thought thy heart had been wounded with the claws of a
lion.

ORLANDO. Wounded it is, but with the eyes of a lady.

ROSALIND. Did your brother tell you how I counterfeited to swoon
when he show'd me your handkerchief?

ORLANDO. Ay, and greater wonders than that.

ROSALIND. O, I know where you are:—nay, 'tis true: there was never
anything so sudden but the fight of two rams and Caesar's
thrasonical[267] brag of—*I came, saw, and overcame*: for your
brother and my sister no sooner met, but they looked; no sooner

---

[266] Oliver has before this learnt from Celia the whole secret of who Ganymede and
Aliena are. Hence he calls Rosalind "sister" here, well knowing that Orlando will
understand him as referring to the character she is sustaining in her masked courtship.

[267] *Thrasonical* is from *Thraso*, the name of a bragging, vain-glorious soldier in one
of Terence's comedies.—The famous dispatch, *veni, vidi, vici,* which Julius Cæsar was
alleged to have sent to Rome, announcing his great and swift victory in the battle of Zela
in Pontus, is the matter referred to.

looked, but they loved; no sooner loved, but they sighed; no sooner sighed, but they asked one another the reason; no sooner knew the reason, but they sought the remedy: and in these degrees have they made pair of stairs to marriage, which they will climb incontinent,[268] or else be incontinent before marriage: they are in the very wrath of love, and they will together: clubs cannot part them.[269]

ORLANDO. They shall be married to-morrow; and I will bid the Duke to the nuptial. But O, how bitter a thing it is to look into happiness through another man's eyes! By so much the more shall I to-morrow be at the height of heart-heaviness, by how much I shall think my brother happy in having what he wishes for.

ROSALIND. Why, then, to-morrow I cannot serve your turn for Rosalind?

ORLANDO. I can live no longer by thinking.

ROSALIND. I will weary you, then, no longer with idle talking. Know of me then,—for now I speak to some purpose,—that I know you are a gentleman of good conceit:[270] I speak not this that you should bear a good opinion of my knowledge, insomuch I say I know you are; neither do I labour for a greater esteem than may in some little measure draw a belief from you, to do yourself good, and not to grace me. Believe then, if you please, that I can do strange things: I have, since I was three year old, conversed with a magician, most profound in his art and yet not damnable.[271] If you do love Rosalind so near the heart as your gesture cries it out, when your brother marries Aliena, shall you marry her:—I know into what straits of fortune she is driven; and it is not impossible to me, if it appear not inconvenient to you, to set her before your eyes to-morrow, human as she is,[272] and without any danger.

ORLANDO. Speak'st thou in sober meanings?

ROSALIND. By my life, I do; which I tender dearly, though I say I am

---

[268] *Incontinent* here signifies *immediately*, without any stay.

[269] It was a common custom in Shakespeare's time, on the breaking out of a tray, to call out, "clubs, clubs," to part the combatants. It was the popular cry to call forth the London apprentices. So, in *The Renegado*, i. 3: "If he were in London among the *clubs*, up went his heels for striking of a prentice." The matter is well set forth in Scott's *Fortunes of Nigel*.

[270] *Conceit* was used of all the forms of mental action, and always in a good sense. Here it means *sense, judgment*, or *understanding*. *Wit*, also, was used in a similar largeness of meaning.

[271] In Shakespeare's time, the practice of magic was held to be criminal, or *damnable*, and was punishable with death. Rosalind means that her preceptor, though a magician, used magic only for honest and charitable ends; such a pure and benevolent magician, perhaps, as the Poet shows us in Prospero.

[272] That is, Rosalind her very self, and not a mere *phantom* of her, conjured up by magic rites, such as it was dangerous to practise.

a magician.[273] Therefore put you in your best array, bid your friends; for if you will be married to-morrow, you shall; and to Rosalind, if you will. Look, here comes a lover of mine, and a lover of hers.

[*Enter* SILVIUS *and* PHEBE.]

PHEBE. Youth, you have done me much ungentleness,
To show the letter that I writ to you.
ROSALIND. I care not if I have: it is my study
To seem despiteful and ungentle to you:
You are there follow'd by a faithful shepherd;
Look upon him, love him; he worships you.
PHEBE. Good shepherd, tell this youth what 'tis to love.
SILVIUS. It is to be all made of sighs and tears;
And so am I for Phebe.
PHEBE. And I for Ganymede.
ORLANDO. And I for Rosalind.
ROSALIND. And I for no woman.
SILVIUS. It is to be all made of faith and service;
And so am I for Phebe.
PHEBE. And I for Ganymede.
ORLANDO. And I for Rosalind.
ROSALIND. And I for no woman.
SILVIUS. It is to be all made of fantasy,
All made of passion, and all made of wishes;
All adoration, duty, and observance,
All humbleness, all patience, and impatience,
All purity, all trial, all observance;
And so am I for Phebe.
PHEBE. And so am I for Ganymede.
ORLANDO. And so am I for Rosalind.
ROSALIND. And so am I for no woman.
PHEBE. [*To* ROSALIND.] If this be so, why blame you me to love you?[274]
SILVIUS. [*To* PHEBE.] If this be so, why blame you me to love you?
ORLANDO. If this be so, why blame you me to love you?
ROSALIND. Why do you speak too,—*Why blame you me to love you?*
ORLANDO. To her that is not here, nor doth not hear.
ROSALIND. Pray you, no more of this; 'tis like the howling of Irish

---

[273] She alludes to the danger in which her avowal of practising magic, had it been serious, would have involved her.
[274] "*For loving* you." Still another gerundial infinitive.

wolves against the Moon[275].—[*To* SILVIUS.] I will help you if I
can:—[*To* PHEBE.] I would love you if I could.—To-morrow
meet me all together.—[*To* PHEBE.] I will marry you if ever I
marry woman, and I'll be married to-morrow:—[*To* ORLANDO.]
I will satisfy you if ever I satisfied man, and you shall be married
to-morrow:—[*To* SILVIUS.] I will content you if what pleases you
contents you, and you shall be married to-morrow.—[*To*
ORLANDO.] As you love Rosalind, meet:—[*To* SILVIUS.] As
you love Phebe, meet: and as I love no woman, I'll meet.—So, fare
you well; I have left you commands.
SILVIUS. I'll not fail, if I live.
PHEBE. Nor I.
ORLANDO. Nor I. [*Exeunt.*]

SCENE III.

Another Part of the Forest.

[*Enter* TOUCHSTONE *and* AUDREY.]

TOUCHSTONE. To-morrow is the joyful day, Audrey; to-morrow will
we be married.
AUDREY. I do desire it with all my heart; and I hope it is no dishonest
desire to desire to be a woman of the world.[276] Here come two of
the banished Duke's pages.

[*Enter two* PAGES.]

FIRST PAGE. Well met, honest gentleman.
TOUCHSTONE. By my troth, well met. Come sit, sit, and a song.
SECOND PAGE. We are for you: sit i' the middle.
FIRST PAGE. Shall we clap into't roundly,[277] without hawking, or
spitting, or saying we are hoarse, which are the only prologues to a

---

[275] This howling was probably rather monotonous and dismal. So in Lodge's tale: "I
tell thee, Montanus, in courting Phoebe thou barkest with the wolves of Syria against the
moon." Wolves held their ground in Ireland until a recent period. In Spenser's *View of
the State of Ireland*, 1596, we have the following: "Also the Scythians said, that they
were once every year turned into wolves, and so is it written of the Irish: though Mr.
Camden in a better sense doth suppose it was a disease, called Lycanthropia, so named of
the wolf."

[276] "To be a woman of the world" was to be a *married* woman, as opposed to being
a woman of the *Church*, which implied a vow of perpetual celibacy. So we have the
phrase of "going to the world," for getting married, in contradistinction to becoming a
monk or a nun.

[277] "Shall we *strike* into it *directly?*" *Round*, in the sense of *downright* or
straightforward, occurs very often.

bad voice?
SECOND PAGE. I'faith, i'faith; and both in a tune, like two gipsies on a horse.

SONG.

It was a lover and his lass,
With a hey, and a ho, and a hey nonino,[278]
That o'er the green corn-field did pass
In the spring time, the only pretty ring time,[279]
When birds do sing, hey ding a ding, ding:
Sweet lovers love the spring.

Between the acres of the rye,
With a hey, and a ho, and a hey nonino,
These pretty country folks would lie,
In the spring time, the only pretty ring time,
When birds do sing, hey ding a ding, ding:
Sweet lovers love the spring.

This carol they began that hour,
With a hey, and a ho, and a hey nonino,
How that a life was but a flower,
In the spring time, the only pretty ring time,
When birds do sing, hey ding a ding, ding:
Sweet lovers love the spring.

And therefore take the present time,
With a hey, and a ho, and a hey nonino,
For love is crownèd with the prime,
In the spring time, the only pretty ring time,
When birds do sing, hey ding a ding, ding:
Sweet lovers love the spring.

TOUCHSTONE. Truly, young gentlemen, though there was no great matter[280] in the ditty, yet the note was very untimeable.
FIRST PAGE. You are deceived, sir; we kept time, we lost not our time.

---

[278] Coverdale, in the Preface to his *Holy Psalms*, speaks of these meaningless burdens of songs: "And if women, sitting at their rocks, or spinning at the wheels, had none other songs to pass their time withal, than such as Moses' sister, Elkanah's wife, Debora, and Mary the mother of Christ, have sung before them, they should be better occupied than with *hey nony nony, hey troly loly*, and such like phantasies."

[279] *Ring-time* is time of marriage, or of making love; probably so called from the use of rings in the plighting of troth.

[280] *Matter* here stands, apparently, for *sense* or *meaning*.

TOUCHSTONE. By my troth, yes; I count it but time lost to hear such a foolish song. God b' wi'[281] you; and God mend your voices!— Come, Audrey. [*Exeunt.*]

SCENE IV.

Another Part of the Forest.

[*Enter* DUKE SENIOR, AMIENS, JAQUES, ORLANDO, OLIVER, *and* CELIA *as* ALIENA.]

DUKE SENIOR. Dost thou believe, Orlando, that the boy
    Can do all this that he hath promised?
ORLANDO. I sometimes do believe and sometimes do not:
    As those that fear they hope, and know they fear.[282]

[*Enter* ROSALIND, SILVIUS, *and* PHEBE.]

ROSALIND. Patience once more, whiles our compact is urged.—
    [*To the* DUKE.] You say, if I bring in your Rosalind,
    You will bestow her on Orlando here?
DUKE SENIOR. That would I, had I kingdoms to give with her.
ROSALIND. [*To* ORLANDO.] And you say you will have her when I
    bring her?
ORLANDO. That would I, were I of all kingdoms king.
ROSALIND. [*To* PHEBE.] You say you'll marry me, if I be willing?
PHEBE. That will I, should I die the hour after.
ROSALIND. But if you do refuse to marry me,
    You'll give yourself to this most faithful shepherd?
PHEBE. So is the bargain.
ROSALIND. [*To* SILVIUS.] You say that you'll have Phebe, if she
    will?
SILVIUS. Though to have her and death were both one thing.
ROSALIND. I have promis'd to make all this matter even.
    Keep you your word, O Duke, to give your daughter;—
    You yours, Orlando, to receive his daughter;—
    Keep your word, Phebe, that you'll marry me;
    Or else, refusing me, to wed this shepherd:—

---

[281] *God b' wi' you* is an old contraction of *God be with you*, which was used a good deal in Shakespeare's time, and has occurred twice before in this play; on page 42 and page 54. The phrase has been still further contracted into *good bye.*

[282] The meaning appears to be, "As those that fear lest they may believe a thing because they wish it true, and at the same time know that this fear is no better ground of action than their hope." Who has not sometime caught himself in a similar perplexity of hope and fear?

Keep your word, Silvius, that you'll marry her
If she refuse me:—and from hence I go,
To make these doubts all even. [*Exeunt* ROSALIND *and* CELIA.]
DUKE SENIOR. I do remember in this shepherd-boy
Some lively touches of my daughter's favour.
ORLANDO. My lord, the first time that I ever saw him
Methought he was a brother to your daughter:[283]
But, my good lord, this boy is forest-born,
And hath been tutor'd in the rudiments
Of many desperate studies by his uncle,
Whom he reports to be a great magician,
Obscurèd in the circle of this forest.
JAQUES. There is, sure, another flood toward, and these couples are
coming to the ark. Here comes a pair of very strange beasts which
in all tongues are called fools.

[*Enter* TOUCHSTONE *and* AUDREY.]

TOUCHSTONE. Salutation and greeting to you all![284]
JAQUES. Good my lord, bid him welcome. This is the motley-minded
gentleman that I have so often met in the forest: he hath been a
courtier, he swears.
TOUCHSTONE. If any man doubt that, let him put me to my
purgation.[285] I have trod a measure;[286] I have flattered a lady; I
have been politic with my friend, smooth with mine enemy; I have
undone three tailors;[287] I have had four quarrels, and like to have
fought one.
JAQUES. And how was that ta'en up?[288]
TOUCHSTONE. Faith, we met, and found the quarrel was upon the

---

[283] This aptly shows the danger Rosalind has been in, of being discovered notwithstanding her disguise. Doubtless, we have all found how one face will sometimes remind us of another by tricks of association too subtle for our tracing; so that we seem at the same time to know and not to know the stranger.

[284] Touchstone is humorously affecting the stately manners and language of the Court.

[285] "Put me under oath, make me swear to the truth of the matter." People were often called upon or permitted to *purge*, that is, *clear* themselves of imputed guilt by thus affirming their innocence under oath. Sometimes a man got others to swear with him, who were called *compurgators*. See page 16, note 64.

[286] The *measure* was a grave, solemn dance, with a slow and measured step, somewhat like a *minuet*, and therefore well comporting with the dignity of the Court.

[287] *Smooth* was often used in the sense of *flattery*. So in *Richard III.*, i. 3: "I cannot flatter, and speak fair, smile in men's faces, smooth, deceive, and cog." Touchstone means to imply, that to use sharp practice on one's friend, to cajole and beguile one's enemy, and to bankrupt one's tailors by running up huge accounts and leaving them unpaid, are characteristics of Courts and courtiers.

[288] *Taken up* is *made up*; that is, *composed, settled.*

Seventh Cause.[289]

JAQUES. How seventh cause?—Good my lord, like this fellow?

DUKE SENIOR. I like him very well.

TOUCHSTONE. God 'ild you, sir; I desire you of the like.[290] I press in here, sir, amongst the rest of the country copulatives, to swear and to forswear; according as marriage binds and blood breaks.[291] A poor virgin, sir, an ill-favoured thing, sir, but mine own;[292] a poor humour of mine, sir, to take that that no man else will; rich honesty dwells like a miser, sir, in a poor-house; as your pearl in your foul oyster.[293]

DUKE SENIOR. By my faith, he is very swift and sententious.

TOUCHSTONE. According to the fool's bolt,[294] sir, and such dulcet diseases.[295]

JAQUES. But, for the seventh cause; how did you find the quarrel on the seventh cause?

TOUCHSTONE. Upon a lie seven times removed;—bear your body more seeming,[296] Audrey:—as thus, sir, I did dislike the cut of a certain courtier's beard; he sent me word, if I said his beard was not cut well, he was in the mind it was: this is called the Retort courteous. If I sent him word again it was not well cut, he would send me word he cut it to please himself: this is called the Quip modest. If again, it was not well cut, he disabled[297] my judgment: this is called the Reply churlish. If again, it was not well cut, he would answer I spake not true: this is called the Reproof valiant. If again, it was not well cut, he would say I lie: this is called the

---

[289] This means, apparently, that the quarrel had proceeded *through* six degrees from the original ground or starting-point, and so had come *to* the seventh degree, the "Lie Direct" where nothing but an *if* could save the parties from the necessity of fighting it out. In *Romeo and Juliet*, ii. 4, Tybalt is described as "a gentleman of the very first house,—of the *first* and *second cause*"; that is, one who will fight on the slightest provocation.

[290] This mode of speech was common. "God *'ild* you" is "God *reward* you." See page 48, note 202.

[291] *Blood* was much used for *passion* or *impulse*. The meaning seems to be, that his being forsworn will depend on which of the two proves the strongest, his fidelity to his marriage-vows, or the temptations of his blood. Such is Heath's interpretation.

[292] Touchstone here just hits the very pith of the matter. It is by such strokes as this that the Poet keeps the man, Fool though he be, bound up fresh and warm with our human sympathies. Celia gives the key-note of his real inside character, when she says, i. 3, "He'll go along o'er the wide world with me."

[293] The personal pronouns were often used thus in an indefinite sense, for any or a. So in *Hamlet*, iii. 7: "*Your* fat king and *your* lean beggar is but variable service," &c.

[294] The *bolt* was a short, thick, blunt arrow, for shooting near objects, and requiring little practice or skill. There was an old proverb, "A fool's bolt is soon shot." In the line before, *swift* is *quick-witted*, and *sententious* is *full of pithy sayings*.

[295] The sense of this probably lies in the circumstance of its being meant for *nonsense*; perhaps for what Barrow calls "acute nonsense."

[296] In a more *seemly* or more *becoming* manner.

[297] *Disabled*, again, for *disqualified* or *disparaged*. See page 54, note 230.

Countercheck quarrelsome: and so, to the Lie circumstantial, and the Lie direct.

JAQUES. And how oft did you say his beard was not well cut?

TOUCHSTONE. I durst go no further than the Lie circumstantial, nor he durst not give me the Lie direct; and so we measured swords and parted.

JAQUES. Can you nominate in order now the degrees of the lie?

TOUCHSTONE. O, sir, we quarrel in print by the book, as you have books for good manners:[298] I will name you the degrees. The first, the Retort courteous; the second, the Quip modest; the third, the Reply churlish; the fourth, the Reproof valiant; the fifth, the Countercheck quarrelsome; the sixth, the Lie with circumstance; the seventh, the Lie direct. All these you may avoid but the Lie Direct; and you may avoid that too with an *if.* I knew when seven justices could not take up a quarrel; but when the parties were met themselves, one of them thought but of an *if,* as: *If you said so, then I said so*; and they shook hands, and swore brothers. Your *if* is the only peace-maker; much virtue in *if.*

JAQUES. Is not this a rare fellow, my lord? he's as good at anything, and yet a Fool.

DUKE SENIOR. He uses his folly like a stalking-horse,[299] and under the presentation of that he shoots his wit.

[*Still Music. Enter* HYMEN,[300] *leading* ROSALIND *in woman's clothes*; *and* CELIA.]

HYMEN.   Then is there mirth in Heaven,
           When earthly things made even
               Atone together.[301]—
           Good Duke, receive thy daughter;
           Hymen from Heaven brought her,
               Yea, brought her hither,

---

[298] The book alluded to is entitled, "Of Honour and Honourable Quarrels, by Vincentio Saviolo," 1594. The first part of which is "A Discourse most necessary for all Gentlemen that have in regard their Honours, touching the giving and receiving the Lie, whereupon the *Duello* and the Combat in divers Forms doth ensue; and many other inconveniences for lack only of true knowledge of Honour, and the right *Understanding of Words*, which here is set down." The eight following chapters are on the Lie and its various circumstances, much in the order of Touchstone's enumeration; and in the chapter of Conditional Lies, speaking of the particle *if* he says, "Conditional lies be such as are given conditionally, as if a man should say or write these words: '*if* thou hast said that I have offered my lord abuse, thou liest; or *if* thou sayest so hereafter, thou shalt lie.'"

[299] A stalking-horse was a piece of stretched cloth or canvas, with a horse painted on it, which the fowler carried before him to deceive the game.

[300] Rosalind is imagined by the rest of the company to be brought by enchantment, and is therefore introduced by a supposed aerial being in the character of Hymen.

[301] *Accord*, or *agree* together. This is the old sense of the phrase.

That thou mightst join her hand with his,
Whose heart within his bosom is.

ROSALIND. [*To* DUKE SENIOR.] To you I give myself, for I am
    yours.
    [*To* ORLANDO.] To you I give myself, for I am yours.
DUKE SENIOR. If there be truth in sight, you are my daughter.
ORLANDO. If there be truth in sight, you are my Rosalind.
PHEBE. If sight and shape be true,
    Why then,—my love, adieu!
ROSALIND [*To* DUKE SENIOR.] I'll have no father, if you be not
    he;—

    [*To* ORLANDO.] I'll have no husband, if you be not he;—

    [*To* PHEBE.] Nor ne'er wed woman, if you be not she.

HYMEN.   Peace, ho! I bar confusion:
                 'Tis I must make conclusion
                 Of these most strange events:
                 Here's eight that must take hands
                 To join in Hymen's bands,
                 If truth holds true contents.[302]—

    [*to* ORLANDO *and* ROSALIND.] You and you no cross shall
    part:—

    [*to* OLIVER *and* CELIA.] You and you are heart in heart:—

    [*To* PHEBE.] You to his love must accord,
              Or have a woman to your lord:—

    [*To* TOUCHSTONE *and* AUDREY.] You and you are sure
    together,

                As the winter to foul weather.
                Whiles a wedlock-hymn we sing,
                Feed yourselves with questioning;[303]
                That reason wonder may diminish,
                How thus we met, and these things finish.

---

[302] Meaning, apparently, if there be truth in truth itself.

[303] *Questioning* for *conversing* or *conversation*. So *question* has occurred before.

SONG.

Wedding is great Juno's crown;
O blessed bond of board and bed!
'Tis Hymen peoples every town;
High wedlock then be honourèd;
Honour, high honour, and renown,
To Hymen, god of every town!

DUKE SENIOR. O my dear niece, welcome thou art to me!
Even daughter-welcome,[304] in no less degree.
PHEBE. [*To Silvius.*] I will not eat my word, now thou art mine;
Thy faith my fancy to thee doth combine.

[*Enter* JAQUES DE BOIS.]

JAQUES DE BOIS. Let me have audience for a word or two;
I am the second son of old Sir Rowland,
That bring these tidings to this fair assembly:—
Duke Frederick, hearing how that every day
Men of great worth resorted to this forest,
Address'd[305] a mighty power; which were on foot,
In his own conduct,[306] purposely to take
His brother here, and put him to the sword:
And to the skirts of this wild wood he came;
Where, meeting with an old religious man,
After some question[307] with him, was converted
Both from his enterprise and from the world;
His crown bequeathing to his banish'd brother,
And all their lands restored to them again
That were with him exil'd. This to be true
I do engage my life.
DUKE SENIOR. Welcome, young man:
Thou offer'st fairly to thy brother's wedding:
To one, his lands withheld; and to the other,[308]
A land itself at large, a potent dukedom.
First, in this forest, let us do those ends

---

[304] That is, as welcome as a daughter.

[305] Here, as usual, *address'd* is *prepared* or *made ready*.

[306] "In his own *conduct*" is under his own leading or command.

[307] *Question*, again, for *conversation* or *talk*. See note 303.

[308] The *one* is Oliver, whose lands had been seized by Frederick; *the other* is Orlando, who with Rosalind is to inherit the dukedom, she being the old Duke's only child. The sense of *offer'st* is continued through these two lines.

That here were well begun and well begot:
And after, every of this happy number,
That have endur'd shrewd[309] days and nights with us,
Shall share the good of our returnèd fortune,
According to the measure of their states.[310]
Meantime, forget this new-fall'n dignity,
And fall into our rustic revelry.—
Play, music!—and you brides and bridegrooms all,
With measure heap'd in joy, to the measures fall.
JAQUES. Sir, by your patience.—If I heard you rightly,
The Duke hath put on a religious life,[311]
And thrown into neglect the pompous court?
JAQUES DE BOIS. He hath.
JAQUES. To him will I: out of these convertites[312]
There is much matter to be heard and learn'd.—
[*To* DUKE SENIOR.] You to your former honour I bequeath;
Your patience and your virtue well deserves it:—
[*To* ORLANDO.] You to a love that your true faith doth merit:—
[*To* OLIVER.] You to your land, and love, and great allies:—
[*To* SILVIUS.] You to a long and well-deservèd bed:—
[*To* TOUCHSTONE.] And you to wrangling; for thy loving
     voyage
Is but for two months victuall'd.—So to your pleasures;
I am for other than for dancing measures.
DUKE SENIOR. Stay, Jaques, stay.
JAQUES. To see no pastime I; what you would have
I'll stay to know at your abandon'd cave. [*Exit.*]
DUKE SENIOR. Proceed, proceed: we will begin these rites,
As we do trust they'll end, in true delights. [*A dance.*]

---

[309] *Shrewd* is *sharp, piercing,* and was formerly applied as variously as *keen* is now. So in *Hamlet:* "The air bites *shrewdly.*"

[310] *States* for *estates.* The two words were used interchangeably.

[311] That is, put on a monk's or hermit's dress, the badge of a religious life. So, before, "an old *religious* man," meaning a member of a religious order.—*Pompous,* next line, is ceremonious, full of pomp.

[312] *Convertites* for *converts.* So in Cotgrave's *French Dictionary:* "Convers: A convertite; one that hath turned to the Faith; or is won unto religious profession; or bath abandoned a loose to follow a godly, a vicious to lead a virtuous life."

EPILOGUE.

ROSALIND. It is not the fashion to see the lady the epilogue; but it is no more unhandsome than to see the lord the prologue. If it be true that good wine needs no bush,[313] 'tis true that a good play needs no epilogue. Yet to good wine they do use good bushes; and good plays prove the better by the help of good epilogues. What a case am I in, then, that am neither a good epilogue nor cannot insinuate with you in the behalf of a good play! I am not furnished like a beggar; therefore to beg will not become me: my way is to conjure you; and I'll begin with the women. I charge you, O women, for the love you bear to men, to like as much of this play as please you: and I charge you, O men, for the love you bear to women;— as I perceive by your simpering, none of you hates them,—that between you and the women the play may please. If I were a woman,[314] I would kiss as many of you as had beards that pleased me, complexions that liked me,[315] and breaths that I defied not:[316] and, I am sure, as many as have good beards, or good faces, or sweet breaths, will, for my kind offer, when I make curtsy, bid me farewell. [*Exeunt.*]

THE END

---

[313] It was formerly the general custom in England to hang a *bush of ivy* at the door of a vintner: there was a classical propriety in this; *ivy* being sacred to Bacchus.

[314] The parts of women were performed by men or boys in Shakespeare's time. The English stage had no *actresses* till after 1660.

[315] The Poet often uses *like* in the sense of *please*; a common usage.

[316] To *defy*, in old English, is to *renounce*, to *repudiate*, or *abjure*. The Poet has it repeatedly in that sense.

51076312R00061

Made in the USA
Lexington, KY
31 August 2019